Stop Abuse and Transform Your Life

HOMEWORK FOR BATTERING INTERVENTION

Kirk Blackard, Francesca Blackard, Albert Chagoya

Copyright © 2022 by Kirk Blackard

All rights reserved

No part of this publication may be reproduced, stored in
a retrieval system, or transmitted in any form or by any means,
electronic, mechanical, photocopying, recording, or otherwise,
without the prior written permission of Kirk Blackard.

ISBN: 978-0-578-39623-1
Library of Congress Control Number: 2022905549

Book design by Jess LaGreca, Mayfly Design

All scripture quotations, unless otherwise indicated, are taken
from the HOLY BIBLE, NEW INTERNATIONAL VERSION®, NIV®.
Copyright© 1973, 1978, 1984 by International Bible Society.
Used by permission of Zondervan. All rights reserved.

Confidentiality

All handwriting inserted in this book by the reader in response to any of the Questions for Reflection or Group Study is intended for that person's own self-analysis and behavior improvement and is private and strictly confidential. None of such writing is to be revealed to anyone else for any reason unless by that writer, or as authorized in writing by that writer.

Contents

Introduction — 1
Part One: Abuse, You, and God: Stop Abusive Behavior — 7
Chapter 1: Domestic Abuse — 9
Chapter 2: Your Story — 20
Chapter 3: Faith — 32
Part Two: Restore Peace: Transform Your Life — 45
Chapter 4: Repentance — 47
Chapter 5: Responsibility—Looking Back — 60
Chapter 6: Responsibility—Looking Forward — 70
Chapter 7: Accountability To God And Self — 78
Chapter 8: Accountability To Others — 88
Chapter 9: Confession To God And Self — 98
Chapter 10: Confession to Others — 107
Chapter 11: God's Forgiveness — 118
Chapter 12: Practicing Forgiveness — 128
Chapter 13: Restitution — 140
Chapter 14: Reconciliation — 150
Part Three: Maintaining Peace: Make Good Choices — 163
Chapter 15: Anger — 165
Chapter 16: Substance Abuse — 176
Chapter 17: Abusive Communication — 186
Chapter 18: Peaceful Communication — 197
Chapter 19: Sexual Abuse — 212
Chapter 20: Sexual Respect — 227
Chapter 21: Abusive Fatherhood — 240
Chapter 22: Positive Parenting — 252
Chapter 23: Trust — 267
Chapter 24: Working Together — 279
Part Four: Future Plans: Plan to Do Right — 291
Chapter 25: Goals — 293
Appendix — 299
Endnotes — 307
About the Authors — 309
Index — 311

Introduction

A *HOUSTON CHRONICLE* REPORT, "SUSPECT IN ex's killing is shot dead by police," sets the stage for this book.[1] Deputies found Reggie sitting alone on a park bench in Houston, Texas. As they approached him, Reggie began yelling at them to shoot him. He then reached toward a bag, at which point one of the deputies shot him. He died at the hospital a short time later.

The deputies were looking for Reggie because he had been charged with the shooting death of his ex-girlfriend, Carolee. He had shown up uninvited at her forty-sixth birthday party on Christmas Eve. He forced his way inside the house and began threatening her in front of fifteen of her friends and relatives, including her college-age daughter. He then told Carolee, "You and I are going to talk."

He took her outside at gunpoint and shot her multiple times. She died at the scene.

Reggie was on the run for several days before the deputies found him on the park bench.

Of the 253 homicides that occurred over one eleven-month period in Houston, at least forty were related to domestic violence. In fact, Carolee was the forty-first.

The Harris County sheriff said, "Domestic violence is an epidemic, and what you don't know about domestic violence can kill you. It happens at alarming rates, all over." He was speaking from the scene of an incident in which a sixteen-year-old boy had shot his seventeen-year-old girlfriend in the leg. He continued, "It impacts children. It impacts neighbors. It impacts co-workers. It impacts first responders . . ."

Can you imagine all the pain and suffering arising in connection with this case of domestic violence? Think first of Carolee. It's not surprising that it was just the last of a long string of controlling actions and violence she and her family had already experienced at Reggie's hands. It probably made her life like hell on earth. Think of her family and friends, watching her suffer over the years and then lose her life to gunshots from someone she may have once loved. Think of her daughter who was there when her mother was murdered. Think of all the others who were affected, directly or indirectly, by her murder.

Although he's not easy to like in this sad story, think also of Reggie. He was so troubled, he chose to commit suicide by cop. One can only guess whether he was driven by guilt for what he had done or fear of the expected consequences of killing his ex-girlfriend. In any case, he was a human being loved by God, who in effect took his own life. He, like Carolee, no doubt had family and friends. His death probably affected them as well as a wide circle beyond.

Remember that the sheriff was speaking from the scene of an incident in which a sixteen-year-old boy had shot his seventeen-year-old girlfriend in the leg, an apparent example of the broad scope and never-ending cycle of domestic violence.

Intimate partner violence affects more than twelve million people each year in the US. According to the Center for Disease Control and Prevention, every minute about twenty people are physically abused by a partner. In their lifetimes, nearly half of all women and men will experience psychological aggression. One in four women and one in ten men will experience severe violence by an intimate partner. Ten million children are exposed to domestic violence every year.[2]

Even for those who are not killed, the effects are obvious. Short term, there are bruises, red or purple marks at the neck, sprained or broken wrists, chronic fatigue, involuntary shaking, changes in eating and sleeping patterns, sexual problems, and other issues. Longer term, victims of intimate partner abuse are likely to develop continuing problems such as depression, anxiety, and substance abuse disorders. Between 25 percent and 50 percent of homeless families have lost their homes as a result of intimate partner violence. Victims of domestic violence are more likely to experience trouble raising their children and suffer family problems than parents who were not victimized. Ninety percent of exposed children will feel the effect of the exposure for their entire lives, causing abuse to ripple through future generations.[3]

Why this Book Is for You

Abusers may be either men or women, and all need help. However, this book is specifically for men who abuse women, which is where most of the problems occur. If you are reading this book, there is a good chance you are a man who is abusive and facing the consequences of your

INTRODUCTION

abuse. Hopefully, you are reading *Stop Abuse and Transform Your Life* because you want to stop the abuse and build a life of peace.

When you abuse others, you usually hurt the ones you love the most. In addition, you probably lose control of your own life, bring problems on yourself, and make yourself feel worse. Your abuse almost certainly destroys relationships and leaves you feeling alone, confused, and lacking self-esteem. You probably do not like who you are or how you have been acting. Your behavior may have been so unacceptable that a judge, probation officer, or other law enforcement official has intervened in your life in an effort to get you to stop the abuse.

Various types of programs are available to help men stop abusing others. Some examples are supervised visitation, batterer intervention programs, peer and alternative support communities, and judicial supervision ranging from supervised probation to prison. Such programs use a wide variety of activities to help abusers stop their abusive behavior.

Some men who complete a program stop their abusive behavior for good. Some don't stop at all. Others quit for a while and then return to their abusive behavior.

Programs that aim to help you "stop engaging in domestic violence" focus mainly of preventing events of abuse. However, if your goal is limited to stopping abuse, your old habits often return and you abuse again. *Stop Abuse and Transform Your Life*, and the TRANSFORM program, of which it is a part, have broader, longer-term objectives: to help you stop abusing and also build a life of peace. The focus is not just on events, but instead is on a journey that will help you stop abusing and transform—make major, fundamental changes in—your life.

This transformation journey should help you stop abusing for the long term. Think of it as like you are lost and driving down a road in the wrong direction. You may stop at a stop sign, but after a time you start again only to continue in the same wrong direction.

Instead, in a transformation journey, you make a U-turn and go in an entirely different direction. When you come to forks in the road, you make the right decisions and continue in the right direction. And you have a plan to continue to make the right decisions until, and after, you reach your destination.

Stop Abuse and Transform Your Life, and the TRANSFORM program, aim to help you take such a journey in which you stop abuse, change directions, make good choices, and find peace in your life. The journey is presented in four parts as illustrated by four signs you might see on a journey.

PART ONE: ABUSE, YOU, AND GOD will help you understand the problem of abuse, your own actions, and the role of faith in helping you change. More importantly, it will emphasize your need to stop your abusive behavior immediately, as the first step in your journey.

PART TWO: RESTORE PEACE will help you continue your journey by making a U-turn in your life. It presents tools to help restore or improve relationships that have been broken by your past abuse, if doing so is feasible and appropriate.

PART THREE: MAINTAIN PEACE will help you handle future forks in the road, and choose to live a life of peace without abusing.

PART FOUR: FUTURE PLANS will help you develop a plan for doing the right things to continue to live a life of peace without abusing others.

A journey of personal transformation nearly always takes place through a rational, internal process that makes big, fundamental changes in the way you think and feel; how you see the world and yourself; what you do; and how you behave. This kind of big change involves several parts of people's lives: physical, psychological, mental, and also their faith. *Stop Abuse and Transform Your Life* considers your faith to be a very important aspect of your journey of transformation, and therefore deals with it in some detail. The book is presented from a Christian point of view. It considers God to be our Higher Power. The Bible is used for guidance in suggesting ways for you to transform your life to avoid abuse, focus on peace and love, and attain your full spiritual potential.

The Christian point of view has been used because we think most who read it will have Christian beliefs. The authors are all lifelong Christians. However, we believe abusers of any religious belief, or no religious belief at all, will benefit from reading and studying it. The book does not try to convert the reader to a particular view about God and religion, or dismiss or discount the teachings of the other great world religions. Rather, it condemns the use of religion as a tool for abuse and calls on biblical teaching for principles that will help any abuser stop abusing, make a U-turn in his life, and transform his very being.

INTRODUCTION

This Book Is Your Roadmap

This book is not a novel to read for fun or even a nonfiction story that you might read for information and self-improvement. Instead, it is a road map for stopping abuse and creating a U-turn in your life. Therefore, it is not to be "read" like you might read other books. Instead, it should be studied, thought about, and made an important part of your way of life.

Ideally, you will use *Stop Abuse and Transform Your Life* as a study and discussion guide in a program involving small-group discussions; perhaps a Battering Intervention and Prevention Program (BIPP), a church group, or other group of individuals who share common experiences and aspirations. If this is the case, you should follow the guidance of your group leader and be a contributing member of the group. If you are not participating in a group study, we suggest the following:

- Read the book as you would a daily devotional rather than an easy read. Set aside a specific time in your schedule for study and thinking deeply about what you are reading.

- Study one chapter per week, no more and no less. This will discipline you to complete the experience in twenty-four weeks while allowing time for study and reflection.

- For each chapter, read and think about the Learning Objectives and the written narratives. Then write answers to "Questions for Reflection or Group Study." If you are concerned about possible legal implications of an answer, consider writing that answer on a separate paper for separate handling.

- Think of your written answers as a journal. Reread, review, and rethink them from time to time.

- Build your learnings into your day-to-day life.

You may wish to involve the victim(s) of your abuse in your study by discussing your thinking with her/them. Under the right circumstances, this can have value. However, you should discuss it with your spouse only when legally permissible, with great consideration and care, and only if she voluntarily and willingly participates.

We encourage you to make the best of this opportunity to stop abuse and make a U-turn in your life.

Commit to Change

When you're relied on abuse, involving threats, intimidation, and violence, to get what you wanted in the past, to change your life and choose a new path will sometimes feel like a challenge. As you begin the process of transformation for the long term, think about how you will choose to behave—beginning immediately—as you learn to live without abuse and violence. Commit, from this day forward, to not using violence against your current or former partner, your children, family members, or anyone that you interact with. Fulfilling this commitment will set the stage for restoring and maintaining peace in your life and the lives of others as you think about and apply the principles presented in the following chapters.

PART ONE
Abuse, You, and God

STOP ABUSIVE BEHAVIOR

CHAPTER 1

Domestic Abuse

> ### Learning Objectives
>
> After completing this chapter, you should be able to:
> - Understand that domestic abuse involves behavior used by one person in a relationship to control another person in the relationship.
> - Identify six forms of domestic abuse.
> - Explain the consequences of domestic abuse, including both the immediate and ripple effects.
> - Provide examples of where abuse violates God's law, the victim's rights, and criminal law.

THE ALARMING DATA BEARS REPEATING: INTImate partner violence affects millions of people in the United States each year.

- About one in four women and nearly one in ten men have experienced contact sexual violence, physical violence, and/or stalking by an intimate partner during their lifetime.

- Over forty-three million women have experienced psychological aggression by an intimate partner in their lifetime.

- One in five homicide victims are killed by an intimate partner.

- Nearly twenty people per minute are physically abused by an intimate partner in the United States.

- One in seven women have been stalked by an intimate partner during their lifetime to the point where they felt very fearful or believed that they or someone close to them would be harmed or killed.

- On a typical day, more than 20,000 phone calls are placed to domestic violence hotlines nationwide.

- One in fifteen children are exposed to intimate partner violence each year, and ninety percent of these children are eyewitnesses to this violence.[4]

Domestic violence occurs in all cultural, socioeconomic, educational, and religious communities. It takes many forms, has many root causes, and leads to many different consequences.

Types of Domestic Abuse

Domestic abuse is present when you use tactics of emotional and physical abuse to maintain power and control over a partner (or other family member) to direct the behavior of that person, and to directly or indirectly cause her to do what you want her to do. Abuse takes many forms, including the following:

- Emotional abuse harms another person's feelings or sense of self and reality when a person does or says things that shame, insult, ridicule, embarrass, demean, or belittle the other person. Examples include criticizing, calling a person names, telling them they are worthless, withholding affection or attention, isolation, ridiculing beliefs, and other similar actions that aim to shift blame for problems in a relationship to victims.

- Verbal abuse, often used to cause emotional abuse, is the use of words or tone of voice to control or harm another person. It might involve actions such as accusing, blaming, name calling, embarrassing, being sarcastic, threatening, insulting, refusing to listen, and limiting another's ability to communicate.

- Spiritual abuse involves the use of religious beliefs or teaching, or biblical texts, to claim God's authority and manipulate people to meet one's needs and do harm to the victim. Examples might include telling your wife that God wants her to be submissive, or that sex is her duty; or molesting children and telling them that God wants them to be obedient.

- Digital abuse, including digital stalking, is the use of electronic and social media such as Facebook, Twitter, Instagram, and others in attempts to control, embarrass, and/or put down another person.

- Physical violence involves actual contact between two people where one hurts another, often referred to as battering. Examples are pushing, pinching, slapping, hitting, strangulation or preventing one from breathing (choking), kicking, burning, punching, physical intimidation, and other hurtful contact.

- Sexual abuse involves controlling a person through controlling the sexual relationship. It may include sexually coercive behavior such as sexual assault or forcing someone to have sex or engage in unwanted sexual acts, becoming angry when sex is denied, criticizing sexual performance, refusing to use birth control, or other actions that make another feel demeaned or violated.

Unfortunately, several types of abuse may occur at the same time. Various kinds have different consequences. They often get worse over time, growing from emotional/verbal abuse to physical violence.

All domestic abuse is wrong, unacceptable, and a violation of the rules and norms of society. Each may be a violation of either or all of the three important codes depicted in the triangle to the right and discussed below.

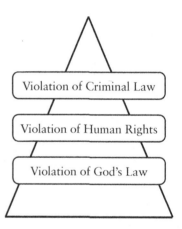

God's Law

All domestic abuse violates God's law. This violation occurs when people fail to live in the right relationship with one another and with God, fail to look out for one another's physical well-being, or fail to behave with honesty and moral integrity. Emotional, verbal, spiritual or digital abuse is not always a violation of criminal law, as is likely the case with physical abuse or sexual violence. However, emotional, verbal, spiritual or digital abuse destroy family peace and are violations of basic biblical teaching and the law of God.

For Christians, these basic principles seem to be summarized in Matthew 22:37–40: "Jesus replied: 'Love the Lord your God with all your heart and with all your soul and with all your mind. This is the first and greatest commandment. And the second is like it: 'Love your neighbor as yourself.' All the Law and the Prophets hang on these two commandments."

This underlying principle of love is given meaning by other biblical principles that point to living lives of moral integrity in a right relationship to one another. They require men to treat women with respect and dignity. Abuse is a violation of all of them, and a violation of God's law.

Human Rights

Violations of victims' human rights involve worse behavior and more troublesome consequences, though such acts may not rise to the level of threats or violence that violate criminal law.

Human rights are generally considered to be the basic rights and freedoms that should be available to all humans. These rights often are held to include, among other things, the rights to life and physical safety, liberty, equality, justice, tolerance, mutual respect, human dignity, freedom from slavery and torture, and freedom of thought and expression. These are the basic, fundamental rights of all people.

Abuse of a woman takes away one or more of the basic rights and freedoms that should be available to all human beings. Therefore, abuse directed against a woman by her partner is nearly always a human rights violation. It involves emotional, psychological, sexual, or physical abuse that denies the woman what she is morally due. It also treats her as if she is less than human and undeserving of respect and dignity.

Criminal Law

The top of the iceberg involves mostly physical acts that violate criminal law: certain threats, and all assaults, battery, kidnapping, marital rape, murder, and other crimes of violence. This category includes the most extreme kinds of abuse.

All states and the federal government have laws—rules for society—that punish offenses against other people, property, the family, and the public. The laws aim to protect individuals and society by making it a crime to use force that causes bodily injury, threatens to cause bodily harm, or causes any kind of physical contact the other person may regard as offensive or provocative.

Violence directed against women by their partner is a crime that violates many of these laws. Such violence is clearly forbidden and nearly always considered serious. Depending on the circumstances, domestic abusers may be convicted of crimes ranging from relatively minor misdemeanors carrying penalties of jail time, monetary fines, probation, or court-ordered treatment programs; up to various degrees of felony carrying penalties of several years in prison and/or large fines. Felony crimes typically include certain types of assault, murder, manslaughter, rape, strangulation or withholding oxygen, and kidnapping. Multiple misdemeanor charges may trigger felony charges.

Causes of Domestic Abuse

Several theories exist as to why men abuse women. All of these theories have at their core that family violence and abuse is primarily something that has been learned, and a man chooses to be abusive even though he could choose to be nonviolent instead. Some of the specific causes most commonly mentioned are:

- Relationships fail and partners hold resentments toward each other, communicate poorly, and learn to deal with one another by becoming violent and abusive.

- A person who abuses another has some type of mental illness or disorder, or an addiction.

- Men have been raised in a culture of violence and believe that physical violence within a relationship is okay.

- Men are considered dominant and in charge, and women are devalued as secondary and inferior. This makes partner abuse a predictable and common part of family life.

Regardless of its cause, abuse involves coercive behavior and is the sole responsibility of the person who abuses. The abuser intends to restrain or dominate by force, intimidation, or threat. Abusers typically are controlling and manipulative. They often see themselves as victims and believe that men have a preordained right to be in charge of all aspects of a relationship. They use power and control that is intentional and tactical. It's like having a hot new car. The man has the buttons, thinks he can make the woman do whatever he wants, and feels powerful in the process.

In summary, various situations may trigger abuse or start a particular incident. For example, as later chapters will discuss, too much to drink or a fit of anger often set off an event of abuse. On the surface such triggers might be seen as causing abuse. However, experts agree that the basic, underlying cause of abuse is a man's desire for power and control over his partner.

Consequences of Domestic Abuse

Just as abuse occurs in many situations and takes many forms, it has many different consequences for the victims, whether they are partners, children, family members, or others. Many of the consequences are the result of clear, really bad abuse, while other consequences may result from abuse that seems less obvious or not as serious. But all abuse destroys peace and well-being, and that which appears to be less bad frequently leads to more extreme forms and worse consequences.

Direct Effects

Specific consequences for victims of abuse are almost too numerous to list, but given their seriousness, it's worth mentioning some more significant ones.

- Physical effects, such as bruises, red or purple marks, sprained or broken wrists, chronic fatigue, shortness of breath, involuntary shaking, and changes in eating and sleeping patterns.

- Longer-term health conditions, such as asthma, bladder and kidney infections, circulatory and coronary conditions, chronic pain syndromes, nervous system disorders, joint disease, and severe headaches.

- Reproductive effects, such as sexual dysfunction, various gynecological disorders, unintended pregnancy, delayed prenatal care, and preterm delivery.

- Mental and psychological effects that include post-traumatic stress disorder (PTSD), depression, prolonged sadness, fear of intimacy, anxiety, low self-esteem, questioning sense of self, and suicidal thoughts and/or attempts.

- Improper use of various substances, such as smoking cigarettes, excessive alcohol use and illicit drug use, and abusing prescription medications.

- Emotional and spiritual effects, such as hopelessness, emotional detachment, feeling worthless, feeling discouraged about the future, lack of trust, questioning one's spiritual faith, loss of motivation, sleep disturbances, and flashbacks.

Children who witness or experience abuse are subject to most of the same risks as adults. They are particularly at an increased risk for emotional and behavioral problems such as anxiety, depression, fear, and academic problems, regardless of whether they were directly abused or observed it in others.

Ripple Effects

Listing the direct consequences of abuse actually tends to oversimplify the situation, as an abusive act always has several consequences. Just one abusive act will have effects in many different places, on many different people, for long periods of time. Abuse is like throwing a stone into a still, silent pond. The stone hits the water in one place, but its effects radiate out in a circle and affect the water in many places and for a significant time, often called the ripple effect. This illustration shows abuse in the center, rippling out to affect not only the partner, but others, including the family and society—often over several generations of family members. An example of how this might play out is as follows:

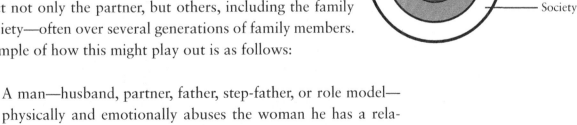

- A man—husband, partner, father, step-father, or role model—physically and emotionally abuses the woman he has a relationship with. He sabotages her job by calling to check on her multiple times a day and leaves her threatening messages. He tries to isolate her from her family and threatens to tell the courts she is unstable and to take the children away from her if she leaves.

- The woman/partner loses her job and feels like she has no choice but to stay with him because she is afraid of losing custody of her kids and wants to protect them from his abuse. She experiences physical pain and bruises from the violence, is able to get very little sleep and is always tired, and experiences depression and anxiety. She feels alone and trapped. She stops speaking to friends and family because she feels ashamed and doesn't know if anyone will believe her.

- The children are aware of what is going on. They become depressed, have difficulty concentrating and develop problems in school, withdraw from friends, and have flashbacks and difficulty sleeping. If they don't find support for the trauma, they may be more likely to abuse or suffer from abuse in their future relationships as well.

- Society may be affected in many ways: for example, if the partner has lost her job and requires unemployment payments, or she loses her home and must live in a women's shelter, or the children get hooked on drugs and end up in prison, society feels the cost.

- And the cycle continues.

Thus, abusive acts do not stand alone. They hurt the main victim and many others, in many ways, and over extended periods of time. Have you been hurt by abuse? Have you abused others? Consider your life story in the next chapter as a way of better understanding what has been done to you, what you have done, why you have done it, and how you need to change.

DOMESTIC ABUSE

Questions for Reflection or Group Study

1. What is domestic abuse?

2. List six forms of domestic abuse, provide an example of each, and indicate whether each is a violation of God's law, human rights, and/or criminal law.

Form of Violence	Example	Violation of
1.		
2.		
3.		
4.		
5.		
6.		

3. Which of the causes of abuse discussed above do you believe is the biggest cause of your abusing women? Why do you say this?

4. On the chart below, list five examples of abusive behavior. Describe the direct effect and the ripple effect of each example.

Example of Abuse	Victim(s) and Direct Effect	Victim(s) and Ripple Effect
1.		
2.		
3.		
4.		
5.		

5. How do you feel and react when someone tries to control you?

6. Why may you often feel it is okay to control your partner? List as many reasons as you can think of.

7. Review your answers to the preceding six questions. List the two things you have learned that are most important in helping you stop abusing.

Personal Reflection

Which of the learning objectives for this chapter is most important to you in stopping abuse and transforming your life? Why?

CHAPTER 2

Your Story

Learning Objectives

After completing this chapter, you should be able to:
- Appreciate how telling your story can help change your life.
- Think more deeply about your life, see the good as well as the bad, and better understand why you abuse others.
- Explain how telling and listening to life stories will help you develop more empathy.
- Use dialogue to share your story with another person.
- Use journaling as a form of worship that brings God into your life.

PERHAPS YOU HAVE HEARD IT SAID, "WE TELL ourselves stories in order to live." This no doubt contains more than a grain of truth. One could also say, "We tell our stories in order to change our lives."

Stories may not seem that important, but our brains naturally tell stories as a way to organize and give meaning to our lives. We become attached to our stories, both the good ones and the sad or painful ones. They become a necessary part of who we are. Recalling your story helps you learn about your history, deal appropriately with it, and change your life.

Telling Your Story

To transform—make major changes in—your life requires you to think deeply about your life story. Telling your story allows you to dig deep, like you are writing a play or a song or doing a rap, with you as the main character and a plot that covers various parts of your life. And sharing your story with others—perhaps when talking with your spouse or significant other, while working with a counselor or minister, or in a small group session with others who are concerned about abuse—helps you think more deeply about your life.

Your Past

Your story includes where you were born and lived growing up, a little about your parents, the names and ages of your siblings, where you went to school, important events, and other facts. But the important parts go far beyond such details, and include why things happened as they did, how you have been hurt, and how you have hurt others, your beliefs and feelings, why you feel a need to control others, your vulnerabilities, your relationships, your dreams and hopes, and other information that reveals who you are as well as what you have done.

Your story will have no beginning and no end. This helps you understand that certain of life's events cannot be put behind you. They will be present as long as you live.

Sometimes you will have trouble remembering things about your life. However, when you tell your story the things you forget (the gaps between the events, feelings, and circumstances that you can remember) will be filled in to form a more complete picture of your life. This will give you a whole picture that you can examine, criticize, think about, and change.

The Good, the Bad, and the Ugly

Telling your story helps you see the good and the bad in your life. Each telling recalls times of happiness and well-being, even though they may be rare and old. Remembering the good times reminds you that a better life is possible. It also provides hope that a better life can be attained.

Your story may also reveal suffering—emotional, spiritual, and perhaps physical—and help you recall how you coped with it. Acknowledging past suffering, perhaps your father's abuse of you or your mother, can set in motion your will to find a better life and help you avoid repeating past events.

You may also describe bad things you have done, including your abusive behavior. Abuse is always unacceptable. Telling your story should never be used as a way of avoiding responsibility by justifying the abuse, blaming your wife or significant other, or pretending the consequences are smaller than they are. Telling your story can help you understand why you do what you do, and how your actions affect others. It can also help you see opportunities for change.

You can see that you are the result of all parts of your story, and that all combined (the past and the present, the good and the bad) describe who you are. How you see yourself usually depends on which part of your story is more important and truer in your mind. Few stories end in major problems, because good usually wins out over bad. Therefore, telling about your life helps you see and focus on the good, the possibilities, and the hope. It can lead to a spiritual conversion or rebirth. Revealing the suffering and bad behavior, and accepting that things of the past cannot be changed, does not excuse your current behavior. However, it does set the stage for dealing with your memories and for changing your future.

The Future

Each story also recognizes that there are future chapters, and that you have the choice to make them play out as you wish. You may never have thought deeply about who you are or why you are an abuser. You may have believed you needed to show off your dominance and never have had a safe opportunity to share your fears and vulnerabilities. Just opening yourself up—warts and all—will give you real power. It can also help you make the right choices in the future.

Dialogue

Dialogue is a conversation in which two or more people exchange information, ideas, opinions, or feelings. The purpose of dialogue is not to persuade someone to do something or to win an argument. Instead, the purpose of dialogue is to explore concerns, gain new insights and understandings, learn more about yourself or another person, or enjoy one another's company. In dialogue, people put their assumptions and beliefs aside for a time and talk freely about the things they want to talk about. Dialogue can be in an organized setting, such as with a counselor or in a small-group BIPP session. It may also be more unplanned, as when schoolmates talk at lunch, friends drink coffee together at a local café, families sit and talk around the dinner table, or people who have hurt one another or been abusive just talk about the past and listen to what each has to say.

Whatever form it takes, remember that dialogue with a partner cannot be forced, and instead should be voluntary and agreeable. It may involve many difficult emotions for both of you, perhaps involving your distorted thinking about your own behavior and her response to your behavior, abuse as a child, or other trauma. Sometimes it may be better for you to seek individual counseling or other kinds of emotional support than to expect that a partner you abused will listen and be open about her feelings. The following sections present some ideas for how you can foster good dialogue.

Talk

Dialogue requires people to communicate in some fashion. People may be separated by miles, or one may be locked up, or they may be afraid to expose their weaknesses. They can, however, nearly always engage in dialogue if they want to and are not prohibited by a court order. There are many opportunities for dialogue. You can talk with your partner almost anytime you are together, or you can make advance arrangements to discuss particular subjects. You can have conversations with family and friends at meals, family gatherings, special events, home visits, or other convenient occasions. You can ask a probation officer, a social worker, or a favorite minister, friend, or relative to talk quietly and confidentially.

Listen and Ask

Remember that the purpose of dialogue is to exchange thoughts and ideas—perhaps tell each of your stories. Its purpose is not to solve problems, negotiate, persuade, or decide, which are often appropriate and necessary in other types of communication.

Before you have a dialogue with someone, ask yourself if you can listen with openness to their responses. Do you have any beliefs about the person that will get in the way of you listening without judgment?

For example, do you tell yourself your partner never listens to anyone and doesn't want to hear what you have to say? If so, you may need to reframe your perspective before you try to engage in dialogue.

Hopefully, in dialogue your spouse or significant other, a counselor, minister, or a small group will listen and occasionally ask questions to clarify, encourage, and sometimes challenge you to be honest and tell your story like it is, without reservation. Listening and questioning is their gift of their time and attention to you. This gift shows your importance. It will help you listen to yourself and make your own judgment about who you are and why you do what you do.

You can promote better dialogue by asking the other person questions. Start with simple questions—that are not sarcastic, accusatory, or directive—and gradually move to questions that are more important to each of you. Show that you want to understand by listening carefully to what she is saying. (See Chapter 18 for more discussion on the subject of peaceful communication.)

Avoid Judgments

Hopefully, you can tell your stories without judging, criticizing, or abandoning one another. Dialogue allows you and another person or persons to come to see each other differently. Often you recognize that you are more alike than you ever realized. It allows you to acknowledge each other as fellow human beings, with weaknesses, emotional pains, strengths, and potentials. Importantly, talking about yourself helps you build strength of self and identify who you really are. Listening to another person helps you understand her point of view and empathize with her, without judging or criticizing her.

Empathize

The private, nonthreatening opportunity to talk about yourselves helps you understand her concerns, fears, and needs. Empathy helps this understanding. You having empathy means being aware of your partner's thoughts and feelings without needing to change them, walking a mile in her sandals, seeing things from her point of view, and being accountable for your actions. Empathy is discussed in more detail in Chapter 6.

When you put yourself in her shoes, you are likely to make a connection. Seeing things from her viewpoint helps you avoid your blinders. When she senses your empathy, she becomes less fearful about revealing herself to you. The telling and the listening allow you to learn from her and think together. They also change everyone involved and help each of you become less fearful, defensive, and self-centered. That is the magic of telling your story.

Journaling

When dialogue is not available, or when you want to be clearer about your story, writing in a journal is an excellent thing to do.

Your Story in Writing

A journal is a notebook in which you write about yourself. You will cover events of your life, what has happened to you, things you've done, your feelings, ideas, hopes, dreams, and other such things. Journaling is a day-to-day account in which you tell your story to yourself.

Journal writing is a great process for discovering and bringing to the surface what you already know deep in your heart. Journals serve many purposes. They can simply tell your story of events or record happy times. They can also prepare you to deal with those you've hurt and fix the problems between you.

Writing about your life, like telling your story to someone else, creates a more complete picture of the parts of your life that are in your mind. The writing usually helps organize your thinking. It also helps you understand what is going on and solve problems.

Writing about pain helps you acknowledges the pain and avoid pretending it doesn't exist. Making lists of all the good things in life can help you deal with your emotionally painful experiences.

Writing in your journal can be a form of worship that brings God into your life. You can use your writing to record your thoughts, thanks, fears, and hopes, while at the same time asking for God's help.

The Journaling Process

All you need to keep a journal is paper (preferably some type of notebook you can keep organized), a pen, and a few minutes each day to record what is important at the time. You can select topics and write all you can think about on those topics. You can write lists of events in your life over a period of time. Or you can step back and describe in vivid detail your personal feelings, reactions, and points of view. Don't worry about how well you write, just keep writing. This is only for you. Most who keep a journal combine these and other practices to write what is helpful and meaningful to them at the current time.

Completing the "Questions for Reflection or Group Study" in this workbook, and perhaps adding additional thoughts on blank pages, makes an excellent journal.

YOUR STORY

Questions for Reflection or Group Study

Use the outline that follows (and blank pages if needed) to briefly write your story and prepare to share it as appropriate.

1. Family: your father and mother, grandparents, stepparents, brothers, sisters, and important other relatives; when and where you were born; what it was like growing up, etc.

2. Important Facts: where you went to school, some of the things you accomplished, etc.

3. Important Events: key things that happened in your life such as moving from one city to another, changing schools, when you started drinking and/or using drugs, any crimes you were convicted of, etc.

4. Experiences: both good and bad happenings that had a major effect on your life, such as an experience that hurt you deeply, an important religious experience, coping with addiction (yours or others), your marriage, a divorce, living with poverty, the death of a loved one, etc.

5. What kind of role model was your father or principal father figure? Explain why you say this.

YOUR STORY

6. Is or was your father or main father figure abusive? If so, complete the following based on your best knowledge of his behavior. (Include yourself if appropriate.)

Person Abused	Description/Examples of the Abuse

7. What kind of role model was your mother or principal mother figure?

8. Summarize your "official record" involving abuse: any cases of police involvement, official charges or complaints, court appearances, incarceration, or other official actions that are on record relating to domestic abuse.

9. Relationships: describe how you get along with your intimate partner or other important persons in your life today.

10. Feelings: your state of mind or emotions concerning relationships in your life: love, hate, fear, hope, sadness, guilt, shame, pride, remorse, regret, happiness, or other emotions; how you felt about important experiences, and how you feel about your current situation.

11. Other: anything else important in your life that you would like to write about.

12. With whom should you engage in dialogue about your life story? What is your plan for doing so?

> ### Personal Reflection
>
> Which of the learning objectives for this chapter is most important to you in stopping abuse and transforming your life? Why?

CHAPTER 3

Faith

Learning Objectives

After completing this chapter, you should be able to:
- Explain what it means to place God in control of your life.
- Understand the common humanity of women and men.
- Describe how love is the biblical teaching that includes all the others.
- List important points of three great Bible codes: the Ten Commandments, the Sermon on the Mount, and the Golden rule.
- Choose to live a life of *shalom*: a life that helps the entire family be okay, complete, and full.

FAITH IS OUR BELIEF IN A HIGHER POWER. Christians accept God as their higher power. Faith is the basis of religion.

Religion is our beliefs about God involving ritual, ethics, and a philosophy of life. Christians believe the Bible teaches about these matters.

We saw in Chapter 1 that domestic abuse involves behaviors used by one person in a relationship to control another person in the relationship. Typically, an abuser wants complete control of his own life and also the lives of others, particularly his wife or domestic partner.

On the other hand, persons with faith that can make a difference turn their lives over to God. They place God in control.

What does it mean to turn your life over to God and give Him control? How could doing this help you stop abusing and change your life?

Turning control over to God recognizes there are things and people, like your spouse, that you can't control. Trying to control people is like trying to play God. Trying to control them nearly always causes harm to them.

Turning control over to God doesn't take away your responsibilities or your choices. You have free will. But you put God's will over your own. You put your self-serving passions, desires, and wants behind you, and instead pursue the things of God. Christians who turn their lives over to God live according to the teachings of the Bible.

Following biblical teachings helps you ask God to change you. With God in control, you will still be you, but you will be more than if you don't follow God. You will be better able to walk away from things or people who hurt you. You will be able to stop hurting others. You will not be free to do everything you want to do, but you will be free to do what you ought to do as you follow biblical principles wherever they lead.

The important biblical teachings discussed below will help you stop abuse and change your life.

Beliefs About the Role of Women

Some of the Bible's literal language—its actual words—particularly in the Old Testament, seems to some people to describe women as inferior to men, and place men in control. Some people believe the story of Adam and Eve in the Bible happened literally as described, and that when Eve ate the forbidden fruit, she fell from grace and became subject to man—and that subjugation fell on all women. Some people also note, for example, that in Genesis 2, God formed a man, but then he realized man needed a helper so he formed woman out of man's rib; Genesis 3 uses the term "rule," "master" or "dominate" (depending on the Bible translation being used) to describe Adam's role over Eve; and Exodus 20 and 21 describe a woman as the property of her father, with ownership transferred to her new husband at the time of marriage. Ephesians 5:22–24, regrettably, has often been used by abusers to justify and excuse male dominance and control over their domestic partners.

> Wives, submit yourselves to your own husbands as you do to the Lord. For the husband is the head of the wife as Christ is the head of the church, his body, of which he is the Savior. Now as the church submits to Christ, so also wives should submit to their husbands in everything.

This and other similar language has been read and interpreted from two different points of view.

Control Viewpoint

The Bible was almost surely written by men. Over the years it has largely been interpreted by men, from a male perspective. Sometimes men use the Bible to justify putting women down, perhaps even abusing them. All too frequently, some men have interpreted Scripture according to their own opinions, and claimed that the Bible condones men dominating women. For example, many men misinterpret the meaning of the word "submit" in Ephesians 5. They apply "submit" to wives, and fail to note verse 21, which refers to "submitting to one another" and later verses telling husbands to love their wives. They then claim that this is an example where Scripture says men are superior to women, and gives men the right to control women.

A simple online search demonstrates that scholars agree that the Bible does not condone or support putting women down, controlling them, or abusing them. They say that in the examples above, the original words meant "serving as an ally, attaching to, or associating with." The following section explains this point of view in more detail.

Theological Viewpoint

Theologians use different approaches to decide what Scripture means. Some look more to history, others more to the actual words, others more to the surrounding world. This book does not take a position as to the best approach. However, it does take the position that biblical writers described the world around them up to 4,000 years ago. They did not consider our current society. Therefore, when reading the Bible we need to look back into the biblical world and try to understand its meaning at that time. We also need to look forward, bridge the gap to our current lives, and decide how Scripture applies in our current world. When all these things are considered, it is very clear that abuse of and violence against women, inside or outside the home, is never justified in the Bible. Men and women are different in many ways, but they are equal as human beings.

The following sections briefly explore three concepts from the Bible, demonstrating that its central teaching promotes peace: peace that is absolutely opposed to ideas of dominance, violence, or abuse. Further, these concepts support the common humanity of male and female. They recognize that men and women are both created by God.

They have inborn, natural abilities. And men and women have equal worth in the eyes of God.

As you read these sections, think about your relationship with your partner and your God. Explore the importance of faith and religion in your personal journey to stop abusive behavior and change your life.

Love

The biblical lesson from Matthew 22, quoted in Chapter 1, seems to bring all the other teachings together. That most important idea is love. When a religious man asked Him which commandment in the law is the greatest, "Jesus replied: 'Love the Lord your God with all your heart and with all your soul and with all your mind.' This is the first and greatest commandment. And the second is like it: 'Love your neighbor as yourself.'"

Thus, love is the greatest commandment. Loving one's neighbor, including one's spouse or intimate partner, is the second great commandment of God.

First Corinthians 13:1–7, so often quoted and so frequently ignored, describes this love. It also shows how love leads to peace, and condemns abuse and violence:

> If I speak in the tongues of men or of angels, but do not have love, I am only a resounding gong or a clanging cymbal. If I have the gift of prophecy and can fathom all mysteries and all knowledge, and if I have a faith that can move mountains, but do not have love, I am nothing. If I give all I possess to the poor and give over my body to hardship that I may boast, but do not have love, I gain nothing. Love is patient, love is kind. It does not envy, it does not boast, it is not proud. It does not dishonor others, it is not self-seeking, it is not easily angered, it keeps no record of wrongs. Love does not delight in evil but rejoices with the truth. It always protects, always trusts, always hopes, always perseveres.

Ask yourself: If I love my wife, and I am patient, kind, not envious, do not brag, am not rude or self-serving, not easily angered, etc., is abuse possible? Not really. This kind of love can only lead to peace.

Two Kinds of Love

We have two kinds of love in our lives. Need-love comes from our own physical, emotional, mental, and other needs. Need-love is our desire to be loved. It recognizes that we are incomplete and often hurting, that our whole being is one of great need. It leads us, often spiritually isolated and lonely, to want God to love us. We also want our families, loved ones, and others to love us. No matter how unlovable our behavior has been, we can look for love with the certainty that God will love us. We can also hope that others will love us as well.

If we accept that God loves us, we want to please Him by living the type of life He wants. Our need for love from others should make us want to improve our lives, because we want to please someone who loves us. We think about our lives and faults, and we try to fix what needs changing. We make a real effort to change in order to please the ones we love and who love us.

The second kind of love, gift-love, is God Himself working through a person. It is the love that one person shows to another. Examples are the love that good parents have for their children even when the children have violated their trust and caused them big problems; or the love a child may have for a father even though the father is mostly absent; or the love most people have for family, friends, and even strangers. And importantly, gift-love is the love that we should have and demonstrate toward our domestic partner.

Lessons About Love

Several important lessons about love can be summarized as follows:

- Love is a basis of all biblical teaching.

- We all need and want the love of God and of one another.

- God loves us even though we do not deserve it, and we should love others even if we don't like the way they have behaved.

- We cannot love as God does if we have our own agenda and always want our way. We should want what's best for the one we love rather than try to control her for our own needs.

- Love and abuse are absolutely inconsistent.

FAITH

Moral Codes

All of us need moral values, or standards of good and evil, to govern our behavior and choices. Believing in God and aiming to do His will offers such standards. These standards provide a practical moral compass for guiding our actions and maintaining relationships with others.

The Bible describes the type of life we need to lead in order to minimize our mistakes, pain, and suffering. It establishes standards of right and wrong, good and bad. It also provides a goal for us to shoot for and guidance in our choices.

The Bible's moral codes are brought together by the great commandment of Matthew 22:37–38, discussed above and repeated here: "Jesus replied: 'Love the Lord your God with all your heart and with all your soul and with all your mind.' This is the first and greatest commandment."

Three great Bible codes that can provide important guidance for your life are introduced below. Challenge yourself to get your Bible and study them in detail.

The Ten Commandments

One of the Bible's great moral codes, or blueprints for living, arose as part of the story of God issuing the Egyptians the Ten Commandments to lead them to a life of practical holiness. He demanded that the people worship no other gods than Him, refrain from making idols or taking His name in vain, and observe the Sabbath as a holy day. He also required them to honor their parents and avoid murder, adultery, stealing, lying, and envy. (Exodus 20)

The Sermon on the Mount

In the Sermon on the Mount, Jesus demands righteousness in our hearts as well as in our deeds. Thus, for example, we are taught not only to avoid murder but also to avoid anger; not to commit adultery but also not to look lustfully on another; to turn the other cheek when someone hits us; and other great teachings that help us address our inner beings as well as our behavior. (Matthew 5)

The Golden Rule

Jesus's teachings demand a good and positive life that honors others and avoids the hurt many of us so often feel or impose on others. These teachings are perhaps best reflected in what we commonly refer to as the Golden Rule: "So in everything, do to others what you would have them do to you, for this sums up the Law and the Prophets." (Matthew 7:12)

Shalom

We all need more in our lives than an absence of conflict and abuse. We need *shalom*. *Shalom* is usually understood to mean peace. However, shalom is not passive or just an absence of conflict. Instead, it's active, with people working to find common ground and maintain relationships that are complete, perfect and full. Other words that have been used for shalom are wholeness, completeness, health, peace, welfare, safety, tranquility, contentment, soundness, prosperity, rest, harmony, and the absence of agitation or discord.

Shalom is a core idea that is the basis for other important biblical principles. Shalom is not a tit-for-tat relationship based on exchanging one thing for another, or what one wants or deserves. Instead, it is a response to needs. The word stands squarely against injustice and oppression. Shalom is clearly on the side of saving the weak, the poor, and those with no say in things. In the Old Testament and the New Testament, the term is most often used to refer to freeing people from physical or political oppression, or personal problems. For example, the term *sodzo* (to save) is used 111 times in the New Testament. The term rarely refers to spiritual matters or sin, but instead refers mainly to overcoming physical or material problems.

The biblical message of shalom promotes change and peace through three basic meanings found in the both the Old and New Testaments: (1) living in right relationship with one another and with God, (2) physical well-being, at a minimum a situation where things are all right, and (3) a condition of honesty and moral integrity. Shalom does not exist where people control others, take advantage of them, or abuse them. Maintaining a situation of oppression, material want, and deceit about the way things are—the absence of shalom—violates what is perhaps God's most basic law.

In summary, biblical teaching requires more than avoiding violence and emotional or psychological abuse. It requires a life that promotes shalom and helps the partner and the entire family be okay, complete, perfect, and full.

Questions for Reflection or Group Study

1. Describe your religious beliefs? How did they develop?

2. What does it mean if you place God in control of your life?

3. One often hears the term "Let go and let God." What does "Let go and let God" mean to you?

FAITH

4. How can faith help you stop abuse and change your life?

5. Provide three examples of the common humanity of men and women.

   a.

   b.

   c.

6. List some ways in which your relationship with your partner will be improved if you show her love.

7. Which specific requirement do you believe is most important for you from each of the following moral codes?

   The Ten Commandments (Exodus 20)

   The Sermon on the Mount (Matthew 5)

   The Golden Rule (Matthew 7:12)

FAITH

8. List several ways you can bring *shalom*—a situation where things are okay—to your relationship with your domestic partner?

> ### Personal Reflection
>
> Which of the learning objectives for this chapter is most important to you in stopping abuse and transforming your life? Why?

PART TWO
Restore Peace

TRANSFORM YOUR LIFE

CHAPTER 4

Repentance

Learning Objectives

After completing this chapter, you should be able to:
- Understand that repentance is a transformation, or fundamental change, in which a person's character and being become permanently different.
- Assess your abusive life by looking deeply at yourself.
- Avoid claiming your abusive actions are justified.
- Transform yourself by changing your attitude, beliefs, and behavior, while you also retain your good characteristics.

CHANGE IS A PROCESS OF MOVING FROM where we are, through a transition, to a new place or state of being. We probably all need to change and do better, perhaps because of things we have done or failed to do, or because we are simply inspired to be a better person.

Sometimes we change the way we act and the person we show the world. But we usually need to change more. We need to make a deeper, more complete change of our whole being. A more basic change of our entire self is called repentance. Repentance involves much more than a change of mind or behavior, or feeling sorry for what we have done. It's not a "quick fix," such as an apology or promise that abuse will never happen again, being a "nice guy" for a time, or attending a treatment program.

Repentance is a transformation—a major, basic change—in which your attitude, beliefs, behavior, and fundamental character become permanently different. You leave your sins and bad behavior behind, and you radically and deliberately change your heart as well as your actions. It is a U-turn, or a 180-degree reversal, that takes your life in a different direction.

Repentance is not a one-time event. It is an ongoing, daily, hourly change of who you are. It's more than remorse or sorrow for what you have done. A sincerely repentant person hates that part of himself that engaged in the hurtful behavior he now regrets. He is remorseful, sad about what he did—not just sorry that he got called on it. Each time he thinks of his wrongful act, he wishes he had made a better choice.

Paul described true repentance as follows in 2 Corinthians 7:8–11:

> Even if I caused you sorrow by my letter, I do not regret it. Though I did regret it—I see that my letter hurt you, but only for a little while—yet now I am happy, not because you were made sorry, but because your sorrow led you to repentance. For you became sorrowful as God intended and so were not harmed in any way by us. Godly sorrow brings repentance that leads to salvation and leaves no regret, but worldly sorrow brings death. See what this godly sorrow has produced in you: what earnestness, what eagerness to clear yourselves, what indignation, what alarm, what longing, what concern, what readiness to see justice done. At every point you have proved yourselves to be innocent in this matter.

In summary, being remorseful and sorry for his behavior should lead an abuser to repent. This sorrow doesn't entitle an abuser to make his partner or anyone else feel hurt or sad or sorrowful. Instead, remorse and sorrow provide an abuser the motivation and opportunity to transform himself, and with the change to see personal and spiritual growth. This growth will require you to take a number of steps.

Assess Your Life

The first step in the repentance process is to look deeply at yourself. Don't just look at what you do or how you behave. Look beneath the surface at what is in your heart. You no doubt will see some good things about yourself: things that are far from abusive and that you and others like. Pat yourself on the back for these good parts of your life.

You probably will also see some bad behavior, including abuse. Abuse doesn't just happen. It arises from an internal system of learned beliefs that falsely tell you your actions are acceptable, even justified or okay. If you abuse others, you probably engage in behavior that is controlling and manipulative, as described in Chapter 1. But you may not see all of the picture, which includes four aspects of who you are.

REPENTANCE

These aspects, your attitude, your beliefs, your abusive actions, and how you justify them after the fact, are discussed next. You can stop abusing if you choose to do a U-turn in each of these aspects of your life.

Consider Your Attitude

Your attitude is your broad, long-term orientation or tendency regarding self, others, and situations. Attitude influences your beliefs and feelings. It also greatly influences your assessment of, and choice of action in, various circumstances.

Men who abuse others typically have an attitude with a focus on "me." Abusive, violent men nearly always put themselves first and consider themselves the real victims in most any conflictive situation. If you are abusive, this focus on "me" usually plays out in one or more ways, such as:

- Thinking and acting from your own perspective and never considering the other person's point of view.

- Meeting your own needs and wants while disregarding those of others.

- Abusing your power and control regardless of the feelings or welfare of others.

- Letting your anger control you without regard to the feelings of others.

- Feeding your addictions, no matter what the consequences.

If your attitude is nearly always to put "me" first, you probably hold beliefs that lead to self-serving actions and abuse.

Think About Your Beliefs

Beliefs are the specific conclusions you make about yourself, about others, and about how you expect things to be. Beliefs are what you think is true, and how you think things really are.

Desire for control, the main cause of most abuse, is no doubt based on your belief that you should be dominate in a relationship. This belief, which may deepen or grow over time, is often driven by several connected beliefs, such as:

- Entitlement: your belief that you have a special status and rights and privileges that your partner does not have.

- Selfishness and/or self-centeredness: your lack of consideration for others, and being concerned chiefly with your own personal advantage or pleasure.

- Superiority: an exaggerated feeling of being superior to or better than others, often used to conceal feelings of inferiority.

- Disrespect, which follows from a feeling of superiority: your failure to acknowledge your partner's abilities, qualities, or achievements—or her personhood.

- Possessiveness: you want to own, possess, dominate, or control another person, and view that person as an object or thing instead of a human being.

- Confusing love and abuse: you try to explain violence as an expression of your deep love and try to convince your partner that your abuse is somehow proof of how deeply you care.

Attitudes and beliefs such as these lead you to abuse women.

Observe Your Actions

As discussed in Chapter 1, domestic abuse involves your behavior in a relationship to control another person in the relationship; to direct the behavior of that person and directly or indirectly cause them to do what you want them to do. When you abuse your partner, you probably use various combinations of the following tactics (described in Chapter 1) to satisfy your sense of control.

- Emotional abuse
- Verbal abuse

- Spiritual abuse
- Digital abuse
- Physical violence
- Sexual abuse

Unfortunately, abuse often grows worse over time. It may start with emotional and/or verbal abuse, and then become physical violence and/or sexual abuse.

Reflect on Your Justification

The attitudes, beliefs, and actions listed do not paint a pretty picture. They often are hard for men to accept. As an abuser, you may think your attitude and beliefs are okay in spite of the conflicting evidence seen in your abusive actions. The mistaken idea that such attitudes, beliefs, and actions are okay may have been encouraged by your having grown up in a family where your father abused others.

When men abuse others, they often try to make themselves feel better by trying to justify or excuse what they have done. They may come up with justifications they think make their behavior seem reasonable. As discussed in more detail in Chapter 5, they often refuse to accept responsibility for what they have done by engaging in one or more of the following thinking patterns:

- Minimize: trying to reduce or keep to a minimum, to intentionally underestimate, play down, or soft pedal the consequences of what we have done. When a man minimizes what he has done, he dishonestly convinces himself things aren't as bad as they might seem.

- Deny: when we hide from ourselves, repress our actions in our unconscious, pretend things didn't happen, or convince ourselves that consequences did not result. Denial means we don't see ourselves as we really are. An example is when you verbally abuse your partner and claim you didn't say what you really said.

- Rationalize: when we allow our mind to construct false explanations for our actions. An example is when you shove your partner and maintain that she deserved it because of the way she talked to you.

- Blame: when we try to shift responsibility to someone else. We see our bad behavior as someone else's fault. An example is when you claim your wife started a fight that somehow justified your hitting her.

Such thinking may make your abusive behavior seem acceptable to you, but it is not. You can deal with these issues by transforming your life.

Transform Your Life

When you look deeply at your abusive behavior and your thinking patterns that lead to it, and help you justify it, you probably conclude that you need to change in some basic ways if you are to stop abusing and bring peace into your life and the lives of your loved ones. Simply changing today's behavior is not enough. To restore peace with God and others, you need to change some very basic things about who you are.

This means changing yourself rather than trying to change your partner: changing your attitude, beliefs, and behavior. The following sections provide some ideas for these changes.

Change Your Attitude

Consider the words of Philippians 2:3–4: "Do nothing out of selfish ambition or vain conceit. Rather, in humility value others above yourselves, not looking to your own interests but each of you to the interests of the others."

As you read the following chapters, think of how your attitude shapes up against these words from the Bible. Consider who you are, and how you focus on yourself rather than others.

Then think about the choices you have and how you can focus less on yourself and more on others. Think about how you can change your attitude from a focus on "me" to a focus on others. Think about how you can change from a "me-centered" life to an "other-centered" life characterized by love for others, and behavior that demonstrates that love.

Change Your Beliefs

Repentance also requires you to change many of your beliefs. Some important beliefs leading to abuse were discussed above. They are listed again here because it is so important for an abuser to change them.

- Entitlement
- Selfishness and or self-centeredness
- Superiority
- Disrespect
- Possessiveness
- Confusing love and abuse

These are the kinds of beliefs you need to change—from a focus on yourself and your own desires, to a focus on others, based on humility, respect, and love rather than abusive beliefs.

Sometimes your abusive beliefs seem below the surface and hard to recognize until something happens. Think of the case of Tony. He often worked late and returned home after his wife and children were in bed. One day he returned after midnight and discovered that his children were sick and his wife was in bed, asleep. The children needed medicine from the drugstore. As was frequently the case, Tony believed he was entitled to relax, and he was focused only on selfishly meeting his own needs. So rather than go get the medicine, Tony stormed into the bedroom and yelled at his wife Helen, "Get out of the bed and go get the medicine. You've been laying around all day and I've been working. Kids are your responsibility—not mine."

Helen explained that she was not feeling well herself, refused to go, and told him to go himself. Tony yelled so loud, he scared the children. Then he pulled Helen off the bed, threw her on the floor, and threatened to kick her.

When explaining the situation to a counselor, Tony said, "She nutted up on me."

Think about what Tony's comment revealed about his underlying beliefs. He demonstrated no respect at all for Helen. He believed that she was acting like a man and resisting and challenging him as a man would, which a woman had no right to do. He cared only about his own self-interest. Therefore he believed he had a right to shove, push, and hit her. To really repent, Tony needs to recognize his beliefs are wrong and change them.

Changing your beliefs that are leading to or justifying abuse is where the rubber really hits the road. If you are serious about wanting to do a U-turn in your life, you need to consider your attitude and what you really believe and then look at those beliefs through a new point of view. Consider them through the point of view of your partner, who has been the victim of your abuse. Seeing the world through her eyes, empathizing with her (discussed in more detail in Chapter 6) will provide a new perspective for you. It will help you honestly consider your thinking patterns, and change those that need to be changed.

Change Your Behavior

Changing your attitude and beliefs should lead to changing your behavior, from actions that control and abuse others, to actions that show your commitment to making your relationship work in peace and harmony: a relationship that reflects love, respect, and shalom.

You can judge your success in changing your behavior by looking at your actions, that you can actually see and assess, not just the attitudes and beliefs that are hidden behind them. Parts Two and Three of this book discuss several situations where abusers usually need to change. Some examples of questions concerning your behavior that can be easily assessed and are addressed in the following sections are:

- Do you take responsibility for your actions rather than use the justifications discussed above? (Chapter 5)

- Do you make or are you making amends for the harm you have caused? (Chapter 13)

- When you become frustrated or angry, do you take it out on your partner? (Chapter 15)

- Do you say or do things that threaten or frighten your partner? (Chapter 17)

- Do you listen to your partner and respect her opinion, and are you willing to hear feedback and criticism? (Chapter 17–18)

- Do you consistently display respectful behavior toward your partner? (Chapter 23)

If you have been an abuser, and you can answer these and similar questions positively, you are taking steps toward transforming your life. Keep moving in that direction. If you don't have nonabusive answers to these questions, you are not changing.

Stop Your Justification

If you change your attitude to one that focuses on others, change your beliefs to foster love rather than abuse, and change your behavior to quit abusing your partner, you will have no need for justification in the form of minimizing, denying, rationalizing, or blaming. Instead of these, you will act as follows:

- No minimizing: You are honest with self and others about what you did and the consequences of those actions.

- No denying: You honestly admit what you did.

- No rationalizing: You do not claim false explanations for what you did.

- No blaming: You accept responsibility and don't try to shift it to someone else.

As noted earlier, helping you make these changes is the purpose of this book.

Questions for Reflection or Group Study

1. Complete the following chart to help you understand the consequences of some of the beliefs that lead a man to abuse his partner. The BELIEFS column lists examples of various types of abusive thinking. In the ACTION column, describe an incident that could have resulted from a man having the BELIEF.

Beliefs	Action
1. Entitlement: I am entitled to control her and get what I want.	
2. Selfishness and or self-centeredness: It's me and my interests that count.	
3. Superiority: I'm better than she is.	
4. Disrespect: I don't respect or feel good about her.	
5. Possessiveness: She belongs to me and I'll do as I wish with her.	
6. Confusing love and abuse: I love her so much I have to keep her in line.	

REPENTANCE

2. What conclusion do you draw from completing this chart?

3. Describe a person who thinks about "me" most of the time and rarely considers others.

4. What single word best describes how an abuser might feel about the way he has treated his partner? Why?

5. Complete the following chart to help you understand how changed beliefs can lead to changed actions. In the NEW BELIEFS column, write what would be a more appropriate belief as compared to the corresponding OLD BELIEF. In the NEW ACTIONS column, write what a man will do if he believes this new way.

Old Beliefs	New Beliefs	New Actions (Resulting from new beliefs)
1. Entitlement: A man is entitled to control her and get what he wants.		
2. Selfishness and or self-centeredness: Me and my interests count.		
3. Superiority: I'm better than she is.		
4. Disrespect: I don't respect or feel good about her.		
5. Possessiveness: She belongs to me and I'll do as I wish with her.		
6. Confusing love and abuse: I love her so much I have to keep her in line.		

REPENTANCE

6. Describe the transformation most men who abuse women need to make in themselves to lead a truly repentant life.

> **Personal Reflection**
>
> Which of the learning objectives for this chapter is most important to you in stopping abuse and transforming your life? Why?

CHAPTER 5
Responsibility: Looking Back

Learning Objectives

After completing this chapter, you should be able to:
- Understand that responsibility relates to cause and effect involving your behavior and its consequences.
- Explain how actions always have several consequences—and any consequence usually has several causes.
- Use "why" and "if only" questions to determine who is responsible for your actions.
- Stop minimizing, denying, rationalizing, and blaming, all of which are unhealthy ways of handling responsibility.
- Acknowledge that you need to choose healthy ways of dealing with your responsibilities and their consequences.

THE WORDS "RESPONSIBILITY" AND "ACCOUNT-ability" are often used interchangeably. It's difficult to define one word without using the other. However, *Stop Abuse and Transform Your Life* uses the two words very differently.

Responsibility is discussed in Chapter 5 and 6. Chapter 5 concerns cause/effect involving actions and their consequences. Chapter 6 looks at what you need to do to meet your responsibilities in the future.

Accountability, the subject of Chapter 7 and 8, discusses answering for the consequences of your actions.

Responsibility can be viewed from two perspectives. It may focus on the past and help you look closely at things you have done, what may have caused them, what the effect has been, and what you should do in response. Or it may look to the future, and consider some important things you need to do in your relationship with your partner and in other areas of your life.

RESPONSIBILITY: LOOKING BACK

In this chapter, we will look to the past and explore the causes and effects of things you have done that are part of your story. If you have caused conflict, hurt, or a problem, you are responsible for it. You are responsible for your abusive actions and for their consequences, including those with a ripple effect involving a series of actions and interactions by various people. You own them, and you should never try to blame others for them.

The story of David, Bathsheba, and David's family from 2 Samuel 11–13 is a good example. David was king of Israel. He was an effective leader who used his great military power to bring peace to his nation, but his personal life was in shambles. He committed adultery with Bathsheba. He then tried to cover up the adultery by having her husband, Uriah, assigned to the front lines of battle, where he was killed as expected. David married Bathsheba, and they had a son, but the Lord made the son deathly sick and killed him as punishment for David's sin. Amnon, David's firstborn son (by another wife) raped Tamar (his half-sister). This greatly angered Absalom, Tamar's brother and another of David's sons, so he had his men kill Amnon. Absalom then incited a rebellion against David, and on and on.

What a mess! What was David responsible for? Was he responsible for Tamar's rape because of the example he set for Amnon and the way he raised his son? Was Bathsheba responsible for her own adultery, even though it was with the powerful king of Israel? What responsibility, if any, did Bathsheba hold for the death of her son? Was Amnon responsible for his own murder because he raped Tamar, or was Absalom solely responsible? Was David responsible for the entire chain of events in his family? If so, does this mean Amnon and Absalom were not responsible for their own actions?

When you are involved in a situation where you abuse a partner, how do you take responsibility for your actions?

Determine Your Responsibility

A man's responsibility for the consequences of his abuse relates to cause and effect. We often think of cause and effect (or consequence) as a very simple, straight-line process, where X causes Y, which in turn causes Z, and so on. But as we have seen, life is not so simple, and cause-and-effect relationships are usually messy, circular, and involve a ripple effect.

Abuse can have several contributing causes. What if your father was an alcoholic who abused your mother and you, was your only role model, you had no support from your mother, and nothing in the system protected you? Are your abusive actions a question of bad parenting, societal neglect, and social conditioning? Who ultimately caused you to be controlling and abusive? Your father? Your mother? A justice system that did not protect you? You? All of the above?

The question here concerns "a cause," and not "the cause," recognizing that several causes can contribute to any problem or conflict, and any action can have several consequences, as described in the discussion of the ripple effect in Chapter 1. And numerous studies have shown that when children who witness domestic violence grow up, they have a greater risk of living in violent relationships themselves, whether as victims or as abusers.[5]

If your father abused your mother and taught you to abuse, or a religious zealot convinced you the Bible said dominating a woman was okay, then the father or the zealot no doubt contributed to your attitudes and beliefs. The situation is a little like a river, with several tributaries flowing into it and often several smaller rivers flowing from it. Several upstream causes influence you to behave as you do, and your behavior diverges to cause downstream consequences to several people in addition to your abused partner. Several contributed to your behavior, and your behavior affects several people.

However, you are responsible for your own actions and for their immediate effect and ripple effects. If you acted abusively, you caused the consequence, and you are responsible. You are a human being with free will, and you are responsible if you were one of the causes. Two tests will help you see your responsibility. You can ask a series of "why" questions and "if only" questions.

Ask Why Questions

"Why" questions help you look at direct and indirect causes of hurt or broken relationships and determine who committed acts that were a cause of a problem. Why did someone get hurt? Why did certain things happen as a result of certain actions? Am I the one who did those things? Asking such questions will help you discover underlying causes of a situation: the basic reason or reasons that, if eliminated or avoided, would have prevented the occurrence. Only if you discover

RESPONSIBILITY: Looking Back

such causes can you identify your role, correct your behavior, and prevent similar situations from occurring in the future.

Using "why" questions to determine who was a cause of a situation involves identifying the troubling event and then looking back in time by asking and honestly answering a series of questions, such as:

- Why does (your partner) have a black eye? Because you yelled at her and hit her.

- Why did you feel entitled to control and abuse your partner? Because you experienced your father abusing your mother.

- Why did you hit your partner? Because you wanted to control her and felt entitled to do so.

Thus asking "why" questions helps you look beneath the obvious and see who contributed to an event or its consequence. "Why" questions suggest in this case that your father contributed to (and also held some responsibility for) the abusive situation. However, regardless of the circumstances and the contribution of others, but for you hitting your partner, she would not have a black eye. Why did she have a black eye? Because you hit her. You were the direct cause of the hurt, and responsible for it.

If you abuse your partner, honestly ask yourself a series of "why" questions. The answers will inevitably lead to you. You are a cause even though others may have contributed, and you are responsible for the situation.

Ask "If Only" Questions

"If only" questions are also revealing. Ask yourself a series of "if only" questions and honestly answer them: "If only I had done or not done something, would the consequence have happened?" "If only I hadn't hit her, would she have a black eye?" Now think of your situation and the "if only" questions that should be asked. For example:

- If only my father had not abused my mother, would I abuse my partner? Possibly not, so my father may hold some responsibility for my attitude and beliefs. However, my father did not take away my free will or my ability to choose whether or not to abuse, so I am responsible.

- If only I had not hit my partner, would she have a black eye? Definitely not, so I am responsible for the abuse. No matter how I grew up, I had a choice in the matter, and I chose to abuse.

Such questions tell who is responsible. If a consequence would not have occurred if you hadn't taken an abusive action, you are responsible for the consequence.

Avoid Unhealthy Responses to Responsibility

Even when abusers, deep down, know they are responsible for abusive actions, they often respond in inappropriate and unhelpful ways. They have a difficult time admitting mistakes, and even when faced with clear evidence of their responsibility for wrongdoing will defend themselves by trying to justify what they did. They try to convince themselves and others that what they did was just, right, or reasonable. They try to avoid feeling badly by maintaining that what they did was not so bad, was the best thing they could do, was another person's fault, or was justified by some other such excuse. They often seem to think that they are the victim—not just more of a victim than the person being abused, but almost exclusively a victim rather than an abuser.

Chapter 4 discussed four thinking patterns and types of behavior that abusers often use to try to justify what they did and avoid taking responsibility for the consequences of their behavior. These are so important in the process of abuse that they will be listed again here. Look again at Chapter 4 to review how they so often are used.

- Minimizing
- Denying
- Rationalizing
- Blaming

If you minimize the consequences of your actions, deny that they are a cause of a particular consequence, rationalize the consequences away, or unfairly blame another, you are not accepting your responsibility.

Do you ever engage in minimizing, denying, rationalizing, or blaming to try to avoid accepting responsibility for things you have done?

The following section offers thoughts on how you can better accept responsibility for your own behavior.

Accept Responsibility

Why bother thinking about and accepting responsibility for currently existing conflict or abuse in the past anyway? Isn't accepting responsibility just a form of "Monday morning quarterbacking" that allows others to criticize, blame, or pass the buck, and leads to your feeling guilty? Shouldn't you just forget the past and move on to a better future?

Certainly, the past is over, and you cannot change what you or others have done. But understanding and dealing with the consequences of your past actions—understanding and accepting your responsibility—is the right thing to do and is necessary for you to deal with what has happened and move to a peaceful future.

Accepting responsibility means acknowledging your own actions and the consequences that result from them: acknowledging that you are the abuser and not the victim. It means focusing on your own behavior and not trying to shift the buck. It means not minimizing, denying, rationalizing, or blaming others for what you have done. When you accept responsibility, you acknowledge what you said or did and your role in the consequences. You change your behavior. You change what you say and do, and not just how you think or feel.

Accepting responsibility doesn't mean hoping for a better past. You learn from history, so you can prevent bad history from repeating itself. If you are responsible for hurting others in the past, then you have a future responsibility for doing something about it. That is the focus of most of the remainder of this Part Two.

You also have some future responsibilities because society says you are responsible for certain things. These future responsibilities will be introduced in Chapter 6.

Questions for Reflection or Group Study

1. Think about the story of David, Bathsheba, and David's family. List three actions that happened that were domestic abuse. List all those who contributed to each act and explain why David was nevertheless also responsible for them.

2. Think about your story as outlined in Chapter 2. Who may have contributed to your lifestyle? Who holds some responsibility for your abusive behavior? Why do you say this?

RESPONSIBILITY: LOOKING BACK

3. Complete the following chart concerning three examples you are aware of in which a man abused his partner.

Incident Description	Responsible Person(s) ("Why" and "If Only" Tests)	Immediate Effect on Person Abused	Ripple Effect on Others

4. What do you learn from completing this chart and thinking about the cause and consequences of abusive actions?

5. Describe an example of how you might try to avoid responsibility in each of the following ways:

- Minimize what happened?

- Deny what happened?

- Rationalize what happened?

- Blame someone else?

RESPONSIBILITY: LOOKING BACK

6. What conclusion do you draw from completing question 5 and thinking about abuse?

7. What are some good things that have happened in your life? Who was responsible for them?

Personal Reflection

Which of the learning objectives for this chapter is most important to you in stopping abuse and transforming your life? Why?

CHAPTER 6

Responsibility: Looking Forward

Learning Objectives

After completing this chapter, you should be able to:
- Recognize that you have a duty to do what is right and appropriate now and in the future.
- Explain why your responsibility includes a duty to serve others with love.
- Appreciate the value and importance of empathy in effectively demonstrating love and dealing with your responsibility toward your partner.
- Begin to put yourself in your partner's, and others', shoes.

CHAPTER 5 CONSIDERED RESPONSIBILITY AS owning your past actions. Responsibility also looks forward. You need to take responsibility for your future by taking control of your life and doing what is right and appropriate.

What is right and appropriate includes avoiding abuse; and supporting, developing, and maintaining a peaceful relationship with your partner and others. With so many relationships and competing priorities, sometimes deciding what your responsibilities are and which should be given priority can be difficult. Part Three, Maintaining Peace, focuses on these types of responsibilities and deals with several important ones: controlling your anger, avoiding substance abuse, communicating peacefully, demonstrating sexual respect, being a good father, and working together with your partner. A couple of overriding principles discussed below set the stage for considering them.

RESPONSIBILITY: LOOKING FORWARD

Serve Others with Love

First, you need to serve others with love. Perhaps the most far-reaching biblical responsibility is Jesus's command in John 13:34–35, "A new command I give you: Love one another. As I have loved you, so you must love one another. By this everyone will know that you are my disciples, if you love one another." This command is such a basic statement of our Christian duty that it is given time and again in various Scripture. Paul developed the command a little further in Romans 12:10: "Be devoted to one another in love. Honor one another above yourselves."

Galatians 5:13 states, "You, my brothers and sisters, were called to be free. But do not use your freedom to indulge the flesh; rather, serve one another humbly in love." This Scripture provides that love involves your own choice to serve another, and should not include an expectation that another will "indulge" you. It does not suggest a man has a "right" to expect love from a partner.

Chapter 3 discussed two types of love: need-love, a reflection of our physical, emotional, intellectual, and other needs; and gift-love, God Himself working through a person. This gift-love, which underpins our duties and responsibilities to others, is often considered *agape* love.

The New Testament alone has over two hundred references to what is considered agape love: that sacrificial love that voluntarily suffers inconvenience or discomfort without expecting anything in return, including brotherly love, charity, the love of God for people and of people for God. Agape love frequently expresses itself as a flow of compassion, an outpouring of care and concern for another person's needs. Jesus exhibited agape love when he fed the hungry, comforted the sorrowing, and healed the sick.

Love Others

We can all show agape love to partners, spouses, children, friends, and others. The care and concern that is part of agape love should lead you to want to honor and fulfill your duties and responsibilities to your partner, your family, and others. Most of these responsibilities are clear and obvious in our culture: for example, avoid hurting them (psychologically or physically), respect them, care for them, help provide for their needs, honor your commitments to them, and do all those things you know from living in our society. In summary, agape love should cause you to make your best effort to never hurt others, and to meet others' needs and reasonable wants.

Don't Expect a Victim's Love

Agape love has no ulterior motive and does not expect anything in return. All too often, abusers have used love as a weapon to maintain control over their partners and make them powerless. Abusers often misrepresent "love" and expect a tit-for-tat, what's good for one is good for the other, response from their partners. They seem to believe their partner should be unconcerned with herself and willing to suffer fear, distress, pain, and abuse, while providing faithfulness, commitment, and sacrifice.

However, continually being abused makes agape love by your partner difficult, and probably impossible or morally unjustified. Just the notion of her offering a suffering, sacrificial love to you ignores and unfairly minimizes your abuse and the hurt you cause her. Therefore you should not expect demonstration of love from an abused partner.

Agape love requires a man who has abused his partner and family to take responsibility for his abusive actions, become accountable, and repent of his abuse—all discussed in this book. For this to happen, you need to walk in the shoes of the victim. You need to demonstrate empathy.

Empathy

Empathy is essential for dealing with your responsibility toward others and transforming your life. It is so important, in fact, that it also is dealt with in some detail in Chapter 2, 7, and 22.

Understand Empathy

Empathy often is confused with "sympathy," but the two are very different. Sympathy is a feeling of pity and sorrow for someone else's misfortune. Empathy is experiencing as your own the feelings of another; when you move into their life with understanding and feeling.

RESPONSIBILITY: LOOKING FORWARD

Empathy requires you to acknowledge your differences, control your emotions, and put yourself in another person's shoes. It goes beyond an understanding in your head of their circumstances, and involves an understanding in your heart and soul. When you are empathetic, you do not try to change the other person's feelings or necessarily understand why they have them. Instead, you try to feel as she feels, see what she sees, and appreciate the emotions that are present within her. You listen, observe, and feel in order to identify and appreciate her feelings. With empathy you are able to see the other person's point of view and react with love and understanding.

Empathy will help you better understand the needs of people around you, and treat them the way they wish you would treat them. It will help you focus on your responsibilities.

Show Empathy

There is no magic formula for developing empathy. The following ideas however should help you empathize with your partner so you can fulfill your responsibilities toward her:

- Listen carefully to what she says and observe her and her behavior to better understand how your abuse has affected her, as discussed in Chapter 18. Ask her about her feelings and beliefs.

- Acknowledge that each of you has different biases and beliefs. Hers are hers, you may believe they are wrong or inappropriate, but they are hers. To understand them, you have to deal with your own beliefs and biases. You cannot understand that your partner is different from you, with different feelings, beliefs, and needs, unless you know who you are and acknowledge your own feelings, beliefs, and needs. Knowing yourself is the starting point for empathizing with your partner and others.

- Control your own negative emotions. You can't see your partner's point of view or meet your responsibilities toward her if you are demonstrating frustration, anger, self-pity, or other negative emotions. If your partner's behavior is challenging you, reflect a minute, take several deep breaths, identify the emotions affecting you, and get yourself in control.

- Try to walk in her shoes. Think about her, her challenges, her fears, her pressures, her level of knowledge, how much information she has or doesn't have. Think about how you might act in her situation.

- Identify with her feelings. When you are empathetic, you do not try to change the other person's feelings or necessarily understand why they have them. Instead, you try to feel as they feel, see what they see, and appreciate the emotions that are present within them. Listen, observe, and feel in order to identify with your partner's feelings.

Fortunately, empathy is a learned skill that you can develop and grow through practice. Therefore, if you are willing to increase your understanding of yourself and others, and demonstrate love, it is never too late to learn to empathize with your partner, and others as well. Your empathy will help you meet your responsibilities toward them.

Summary

You need to decide what your responsibility to your partner or another person is. The answer will be clear if you demonstrate love, feel their needs, and respond to those needs. "Part Three: Maintaining Peace," discusses in some detail many of your responsibilities and how you should deal with them in several specific cases: controlling anger, dealing with substance abuse, communicating, demonstrating sexual respect, being a good father, establishing trust and respect, and working together. As you read those chapters, walk in your partner's shoes.

RESPONSIBILITY: LOOKING FORWARD

Questions for Reflection or Group Study

1. Scripture teaches to serve one another with love. How can you do that with your spouse or significant other?

2. Complete the following chart by summarizing your own beliefs and what you think are your partner's beliefs on each subject.

Subject	My Beliefs	My Partner's Beliefs
Religion		
Core Values		
Financial Matters		
Children		
Housekeeping		
Sex		
Private/Personal Time		

3. Complete the following chart by listing your three greatest needs and what you think are your partner's greatest needs.

My Greatest Needs	My Partner's Greatest Needs

4. Complete the following chart by listing your three greatest fears and what you think are your partner's greatest fears.

My Greatest Fears	My Partner's Greatest Fears

RESPONSIBILITY: LOOKING FORWARD

5. What do questions 2, 3, and 4 tell you about empathy and how you should empathize with your partner?

6. List four of your responsibilities for the future.

Personal Reflection

Which of the learning objectives for this chapter is most important to you in stopping abuse and transforming your life? Why?

CHAPTER 7
Accountability to God and Self

Learning Objectives

After completing this chapter, you should be able to:
- Explain that accountability means being answerable and implies a legal, moral, or other obligation to someone as though they were sitting in judgment.
- Answer to God: develop a relationship with God that promotes your own honesty, obedience, and genuine love and respect for others.
- Answer to yourself: follow your conscience, fulfill your responsibilities, and exercise self-control.

ACCOUNTABILITY MEANS BEING ANSWERABLE and implies a legal, moral, or other obligation to someone as though they were sitting in judgment and can in some way call you to account. You are accountable to someone when you have a duty to them. While responsibility is largely a function of what you do, accountability is based on rules, expectations, or judgments by yourself and others about who you are answerable to. It often is a duty based on relationships and unstated expectations of those you care about or love. You are being accountable when you accept responsibility for your actions and do what is necessary to fulfill your obligations to make things right with those who have a legitimate expectation of you.

We will explore accountability from two perspectives. First, you cannot really answer to someone else until you get your own act together. To do that, you need to answer to God and self. Therefore, this kind of accountability is discussed in this chapter. Chapter 8 will explore your need to be accountable to others, including society, the legal system, your family, and particularly your partner.

Accountability to God

Different religious traditions have different beliefs about what it means to be accountable to God. In this book, we are not talking about pressure tactics, bargaining with God, or complying with a specific religious doctrine. Rather, here accountability means developing a relationship with God that promotes your own honesty, goodness, and genuine love and respect for others. It leads to a relationship that helps you live by faith and your own religious convictions, and do what is best for others.

Biblical Teachings

Being accountable to God is one of the first lessons taught in the Bible—in the story of Adam and Eve in Genesis. Satan appeared as a serpent and charmed Eve into eating fruit of the Tree of the Knowledge of Good and Evil. Eve then convinced Adam to do the same. When the Lord questioned the three as to what had happened, Adam tried to blame his wife. When asked what she had done, Eve tried to shift the responsibility to the serpent. The serpent likewise tried to excuse himself. The Lord, however, held each of them accountable for their actions by imposing just consequences for their individual choices.

Most people of faith believe their blessings come from God. He entrusts each of us with talents—time, treasure, skills, spiritual gifts, and relationships. We all have our own individual ability to use them constructively with love and respect. We also have the capacity to misuse them through neglect, waste, or abuse. And we have to answer for our choices.

The parable of the bags of gold from Matthew 25:14–30 teaches that we are accountable—answerable—for our choices in how we use, or misuse, our talents. It is the story of a man leaving on a trip who gave five valuable coins to one servant, two to another, and one to the third servant.

The servant who had five coins went to work and gained five more, and the one who had been given two coins gained two more. But the servant who had received only one coin buried it, and the value didn't increase.

When the master returned, he settled the accounts and held each of the servants accountable for how he had handled his talents. He was pleased with the first two because they had used their talents and gained more. But when the one who had received one coin came and said he had hidden it in the ground, and returned only the coin he had been given, the master was angry, took the coin, and gave it to the servant who had ten coins. Then the master said,

> So take the bag of gold from him and give it to the one who has ten bags. For whoever has will be given more, and they will have an abundance. Whoever does not have, even what they have will be taken from them. And throw that worthless servant outside, into the darkness, where there will be weeping and gnashing of teeth.

Thus, accountability was a settling of the accounts. Accountability to God is further elaborated in Matthew 25:40: "The King will reply, 'Truly I tell you, whatever you did for one of the least of these brothers and sisters of mine, you did for me.'"

Being accountable to others is also being accountable to God.

Being Accountable

Being accountable to God means that faith guides your thinking and behavior, and helps transform your life. You recognize your gifts from God, like the first two servants in the parable of the bags of gold. You make the most of your gifts by doing for the least and the weak, and by acting with respect and love rather than controlling and abusing. You live according to biblical values such as:

- Building a strong relationship with God, and fair and respectful relationships with others.

- Learning to relate with God more deeply so you can better respond to His teachings.

- Praying about your personal needs and the needs of others.

- Demonstrating love while expecting nothing in return.

- Reexamining your thinking and becoming teachable.

- Being willing to learn about yourself.

- Sharing with other people.

- Becoming more sensitive and discerning.
- Treating others as you wish to be treated.

In summary, if you are accountable to God you invite Him to examine your motives as well as your behavior. You surrender your deepest needs, hopes, and dreams; serve others; and in doing so find food for your soul.

Accountability to Self

Being accountable to yourself is a choice. As an abuser, if you make this important choice and hold yourself accountable for your past behavior as well as for changing and acting appropriately in the future, then you have taken a gigantic step in the right direction.

If you hate yourself when you do something or neglect to do something that hurts another person, and you act to correct the situation, then you are being accountable to yourself. Answering to yourself, or self-accountability, will help you recognize when you have harmed another person by something you've done or neglected to do, and choose to correct the situation with respect, without doing further harm.

Self-accountability is the basis for your freedom. In its absence, you are likely to violate society's standards or laws and eventually have to be accountable to another authority. Your behavior will probably be controlled by others—such as the law enforcement or judicial systems—through fear, threats and punishment, or sometimes by separation from society in prison. And you probably don't want someone in authority to force you to act responsibly and without abusing others. You want to do what's right out of your own free will. That is being accountable to yourself.

Being accountable to self requires you to answer to your conscience, fulfill your responsibilities, and control yourself.

Answer to Your Conscience

Being accountable to self requires you to answer to your conscience. Your conscience is that small inner voice, that inborn feeling, that sometimes haunts you and on other occasions gives you joy. It helps you understand the difference between good and evil. In Scripture, conscience is also called "heart," as in 1 John 3:18–22:

> Dear children, let us not love with words or speech but with actions and in truth. This is how we know that we belong to the truth and how we set our hearts at rest in his presence: If our hearts condemn us, we know that God is greater than our hearts, and he knows everything. Dear friends, if our hearts do not condemn us, we have confidence before God and receive from him anything we ask, because we keep his commands and do what pleases him.

In the Sermon on the Mount (Matthew 6:22–23), Jesus compared conscience to the "eyes" by which a person can evaluate his moral condition:

> The eye is the lamp of the body. If your eyes are healthy, your whole body will be full of light. But if your eyes are unhealthy, your whole body will be full of darkness. If then the light within you is darkness, how great is that darkness!

The conscience has been described as an angel on one shoulder and the devil on the other. Your choice as to which to listen to is your struggle between good and bad, right and wrong, and is a reflection of your moral values. Your moral values, your sense of what is acceptable and what is not acceptable, are largely a function of your parents, the environment in which you grew up, your religious training, and other factors that make you who you are. Your moral values are not static, and can change over time as you live and learn.

Doing what you know in your heart is right—listening to the angel on one shoulder, rather than the devil on the other one—is the essence of being accountable to yourself. It's the kind of accountability that causes you to stop abusing and transform your life.

Fulfill Your Responsibilities

In the previous chapter, we summarized some of your responsibilities to others when you serve them with love. We suggested that your love for others can be demonstrated by committing to make your best effort to meet their needs and reasonable wants. This of course raises questions of accountability to others, to be discussed in the following chapter. However, when you make a commitment to another, you also need to be responsible and accountable to yourself to fulfill that commitment.

A commitment has been defined as choosing to take on and fulfill an obligation or promise. An example is the choice of serving another with love. Doing what is required to serve others with love makes it very personal, involving relationships and emotional bonds that each individual must be personally accountable for. Only you can answer for your personal relationships. And you are accountable to yourself to follow through and be responsible for your commitments.

Holding yourself accountable for delivering on your responsibilities includes following through and doing what you know you should do, what you say you will do, when you should do it. This, in turn, helps you build trust, the confident belief that someone will do what you expect them to do, as discussed in more detail in Chapter 23. There will be little trust if you do not answer to yourself to ensure that you fulfill your responsibilities to others.

A key factor in being accountable to self by delivering on your responsibilities to others is empathy. Chapter 6, "Responsibility: Looking Forward," described empathy in some detail. It largely grows out of the Golden Rule of Matthew 7:12, "So in everything, do to others what you would have them do to you, for this sums up the Law and the Prophets."

Empathy helps you determine what your responsibilities to others are. This means really listening to what people say and observing what they do. You then walk in their shoes before deciding how you should honor your commitments to them—and be accountable to yourself.

Control Yourself

The question of control can be seen from different perspectives. Chapter 1 noted that abusers nearly always choose to try to control the lives of others, particularly their wives or domestic partners. Chapter 3 noted that persons of deep faith turn their lives over to God, and place God in control. Here we will see that to be accountable to yourself, you also need to control your own choices and actions.

Self-control is the ability to control your thinking, your decision making, and your behavior. Sometimes it is called self-discipline. It also is being accountable to self. It enables you to follow God's teachings and say "no" and "enough" to yourself. It helps you get beyond your desire to control others, and stop doing things that are harmful to others and to you. Being accountable to yourself puts you, hopefully with God's guidance, in control of your life and your behavior.

As an abuser, you probably need to deal with the areas of your life that seem to run off track and need changing. However, you should really focus on stopping your attempts to control others. Identify the thoughts and beliefs that push you to try to control them. Think about the consequences of your behavior and how your life and the lives of others would be better if you focused on controlling yourself—being accountable to yourself—rather than on controlling others.

Questions for Reflection or Group Study

1. List several of your blessings.

2. What have you done with those blessings?

3. How do you think your faith, or lack of faith, will affect your accountability to God?

4. What have been the main factors that influenced your conscience and caused it to be what it is?

5. Explain how your conscience should guide your behavior.

6. How is serving others a form of self-accountability?

7. What can you do to be accountable to self?

> **Personal Reflection**
>
> Which of the learning objectives for this chapter is most important to you in stopping abuse and transforming your life? Why?

CHAPTER 8

Accountability to Others

Learning Objectives

After completing this chapter, you should be able to:
- Explain that accountability means answering for your responsibilities and recognizing your obligation to make things right with those who have a legitimate expectation of you.
- List the main people or entities you are accountable to.
- Identify what behavior and actions you are accountable for.
- Demonstrate that you are accountable for your past abuse.

AN ARTICLE IN *THE HOUSTON CHRONICLE* ENTI-
tled "Man gets 15 years for slapping girlfriend" reads as follows:

> A [local] man will spend the next 15 years in prison for slapping his girlfriend after she didn't bring home food from Jack in the Box for him.
>
> A Montgomery County jury found [name], 33, guilty of assault family violence on Feb. 28 after 40 minutes of deliberation. [Name] had previous convictions of assault family violence, prosecutors said.
>
> The incident happened at the couple's home . . . on Independence Day. [Name] had texted his 29-year-old girlfriend, asking her to bring home food from the fast-food restaurant.
>
> Prosecutors said the girlfriend did not see the text and came home instead of stopping for food. Angered, [name] slapped her across the face. The girlfriend was holding the couple's baby at the time of the assault. [Name] grabbed the baby and took off with the woman's car and phone. The woman made it to her

mother's home and called 911. She returned home while on the phone with 911, at which time [name] showed up again.[6]

This man will be eligible for parole after a long prison sentence. He learned about accountability the hard way. He failed to be accountable to God, himself, his girlfriend, or others, so the state took charge. The state held him accountable.

As discussed in Chapter 7, accountability to God and self is a personal, private matter. But accountability to others is different, usually involving several people and expectations from various sources. You are being accountable when you accept responsibility for your actions and acknowledge your obligation to respect the valid needs, expectations, or rights of others.

Accountability cuts both ways. It is both mutual and individual. From a mutual perspective, when you have a relationship with another, you are accountable to one another. Mutual accountability is the glue that holds relationships together, or the magnet that pulls people toward one another when relationships are being built or repaired. However, individually, each person in the relationship is responsible for evaluating their personal circumstances and making their own choices about who they are accountable to, and for what. One person can decide to be accountable to another, but cannot force the other to be accountable to him or her. You are being accountable to your partner when you respect her right to control her own life, honor your marriage vows or other promises, do what you say you will do on a daily basis, do your part in effectively managing your finances, are a good father to your children, communicate honestly and openly, and make an honest effort to do the many other things that she might reasonably expect.

Outlined below are thoughts as to who you should be accountable to, what you are accountable for, and your continuing accountability for past actions.

Who You Are Accountable To

We all have a duty to answer for our actions. This accountability arises from a contract or agreement—sometimes formal and written, but usually unstated and often unacknowledged—that we have with other people, entities, and society. It may arise from a formal relationship, such as your obligations under the law (as Steven learned), or by specific, written contract. For example, you are answerable to the state to obey its laws (just as Steven was) and to creditors to repay loans.

More often, however, accountability is informal, based on relationships and unstated expectations of those you care about or love and those who care about or love you. These relationships determine what can reasonably be expected of you and another person. They establish, perhaps informally, each of your rights and obligations: what you can expect from another person, and what the other should be able to expect from you. Accountability follows the expectations.

You are accountable to those who have reasonable expectations of you and to whom you are obligated to fulfill those expectations. For example, you probably are accountable to:

- Your partner, probably because of social norms, religious teachings, and/or promises you made at the time of your marriage or other commitment.

- Your family: children, parents, siblings, and others, probably because of what society expects, religious teachings, and sometimes because of legal requirements.

- Your boss, perhaps because of an informal or formal employment contract.

- The legal system, and in particular the judge, probation officer, or other entities to whom you may be required to report.

- Strangers, because you need to do the right thing, and the law provides others various protections.

- Society at large, because of society's expectations as expressed primarily through how things generally work in the particular culture.

You probably can think of others you are answerable to as well.

Your Accountability for Future Actions

Chapter 6 discussed your continuing responsibility to your partner and other people, and the section above discussed the broad range of people to whom you are accountable. You are accountable for what you are responsible for, and for what you have done and will do with respect to those responsibilities.

This book will not address your accountability to all the people to whom you are responsible, such as your siblings, your boss, society, and others mentioned above. Their expectations are usually clear, and understanding those expectations usually defines your accountability to them.

Our focus here is your accountability to your domestic partner. You need to demonstrate love, feel your partner's needs, and respond to them. You can do this by taking control of your own personal life—not your partner's—and doing things that are morally right and legally required; that avoid abuse, develop and maintain a loving, peaceful relationship; and that fulfill her reasonable needs regarding issues such as your financial obligations and a safe, stable life. Part Three: Maintaining Peace discusses in some detail many of your responsibilities—and therefore, your accountability—in several specific cases: controlling anger, dealing with substance abuse, communicating, demonstrating sexual respect, being a good father, establishing trust and respect, and working together.

In summary, you are accountable—answerable—to your partner to meet your obligations and commitments in all these areas. Being accountable means you do what is reasonably necessary to fulfill them.

Your Accountability for Past Abuse

As discussed in Chapter 5, if you have abused a partner, failed to meet her reasonable expectations, or otherwise acted inappropriately in the past, you are responsible for the consequences. Similarly, you are accountable for your past inappropriate actions, and you need to answer for those actions and make good for the damage you've done. As discussed above, your partner can then choose how to respond to your offer of accountability.

Why You Are Accountable

Abuse of another person, physical or otherwise, is always inappropriate. Thinking about the following will help you see how inappropriate it is and why you are accountable for your abuse of others.

- Your actions hurt other people. Honestly considering the consequences of your abuse will help you see that it is wrong and that you need to answer for it.

- You probably feel bad about it. Most people have a pretty good understanding of right and wrong, good and bad, and you probably do as well. You know whether your actions show love, kindness, generosity, altruism, or justice; or whether they show desire for control, self-interest, one-upmanship, or exploitation of someone who doesn't have power or a voice. When you have been abusive, you probably know it, and you need to answer for it.

- Abuse is inconsistent with the teachings of the Christian tradition. In Chapter 3, we briefly discussed some great moral codes of Christianity: the Ten Commandments, the Sermon on the Mount, and the Golden Rule. These, or other principles of your religious tradition, are guideposts that provide a blueprint for living and help you distinguish right from wrong, good from bad.

- Your abuse violates the law. Laws are generally established to protect a larger group or society at large from the acts of an individual. Your abusive acts nearly always harm a larger group as well as your individual victim, and violate the law. If you are violating a law, your actions are almost surely inappropriate and you will have to answer for them.

- You had a choice in the matter. Notions of accountability for actions are intimately related to notions of free will: to questions of whether your actions are inevitable and not determined by you, or whether you have choices about your actions. Men sometimes claim they are not acting freely when family and parental influences—say, an abusive childhood—negatively affect their behavior. However, while such external factors may influence you toward abuse, they do not force you to do what you do. And they don't prevent you from doing what you ought to do. You are free, and able to choose your own course of action. You are free if you have the final choice, even if experiences from earlier life, like seeing your father abuse your mother, make your choice more difficult.

Think about these issues and how they fit in your case. If you abused another person, you are accountable. So, what do you do?

How You Are Accountable

To be accountable for past abuse, you need to make things right—as discussed in several of the chapters that follow. You need to start by "confessing," discussed in some detail in the following chapter and briefly introduced below.

Being accountable by confessing means that when you make a mistake, you own up to your actions and "come clean." You admit that the mistake was indeed your fault. You go to the person you hurt and say things such as:

- "I made a mistake when I _____."
- "I screwed up."
- "That's on me, and no one else."
- "No excuses."
- "I'll accept it—it's mine."
- "I got it."

Note that these statements of accountability make heavy use of the pronoun "I." They don't hide behind "we" or "they" or blame others. They take personal accountability by being specific about the choices you decided on and the consequences of those choices.

Being accountable starts with looking in the mirror. When we screw up, we often tend to blame external circumstances. Accountability means we blame our mistakes on the person we see in the mirror, without whining, finger-pointing, blaming, or making excuses.

While being accountable involves admitting our mistakes, doing that is only part of the story. We need to learn from our mistakes and correct our behavior. There are a number of ways to do this, most considered in other chapters of this book. As you consider other chapters, think about how they can help you be accountable to your partner and others by changing your life and avoiding abuse in the future.

Questions for Reflection or Group Study

1. What is the relationship between responsibility and accountability?

2. List five persons or entities you should be accountable to and what your duty to them is.

Person/Entity	Duty

3. Repentance means making a major change in who you are and in your life. How does accountability relate to repentance?

4. Do you have a choice in how you treat your partner? If you answer "no," what prevents you from having a choice? If you answer "yes," what factors do you consider when you choose how to treat her?

5. Write an accountability statement (on a separate sheet of paper if you wish) by answering the following:

    - Describe your abusive/violent behavior toward the victim. (Describe "what" you did, not "why" you did it, and use the victim's first name.)

- Describe how your abusive/violent behavior has affected her. (Do not include yourself.)

- Describe how your abusive/violent behavior has affected others, such as children, friends, family, coworkers, etc. (Do not include yourself.)

6. What should you do to demonstrate your accountability?

Personal Reflection

Which of the learning objectives for this chapter is most important to you in stopping abuse and transforming your life? Why?

CHAPTER 9

Confession to Self and God

Learning Objectives

After completing this chapter, you should be able to:
- Explain that confessing means admitting you have been wrong and acknowledging or disclosing your misdeeds, faults, or sins.
- Confess to yourself by honestly answering to your conscience for what you have done.
- Confess to God in your own special way, according to the dictates of your spiritual tradition.

THE STORY OF THE PRODIGAL SON FROM LUKE 15:11–24 teaches many lessons and includes a wonderful example of the act of confession.

> Jesus continued: "There was a man who had two sons. The younger one said to his father, 'Father, give me my share of the estate.' So he divided his property between them. Not long after that, the younger son got together all he had, set off for a distant country and there squandered his wealth in wild living.
>
> After he had spent everything, there was a severe famine in that whole country, and he began to be in need. So he went and hired himself out to a citizen of that country, who sent him to his fields to feed pigs. He longed to fill his stomach with the pods that the pigs were eating, but no one gave him anything. When he came to his senses, he said, "How many of my father's hired servants have food to spare, and here I am starving to death! I will set out and go back to my father and say to him: Father, I have sinned against heaven and against you. I am no longer worthy to be

called your son; make me like one of your hired servants." So he got up and went to his father.

But while he was still a long way off, his father saw him and was filled with compassion for him; he ran to his son, threw his arms around him and kissed him. The son said to him, "Father, I have sinned against heaven and against you. I am no longer worthy to be called your son." But the father said to his servants, "Quick! Bring the best robe and put it on him. Put a ring on his finger and sandals on his feet. Bring the fattened calf and kill it. Let's have a feast and celebrate. For this son of mine was dead and is alive again; he was lost and is found." So they began to celebrate.

Look at what the lost son did:

- He confessed to himself. When he came to his senses, he said, "I'm starving to death," and he saw the need to get up and go to his father and confess.

- He confessed to his father, saying, "Father, I have sinned against heaven and against you." Biblical scholars commonly suggest that the father in this story also represents the heavenly Father, to whom the son confessed.

The prodigal son confessed to himself and to God. Confessing to yourself and to God will be discussed in this chapter. He also confessed to his human father, the person he had hurt. Confessing to those people you have hurt will be discussed in Chapter 10.

Purpose of Confession

Confessing means admitting you have been wrong and acknowledging or disclosing your misdeeds, faults, or sins. You make a good, ol' fashioned apology. When you admit you make mistakes and are flawed, you confirm your honesty, your morality, your strength, and your dignity.

Confession usually follows from accepting responsibility. It's a logical next step, the "proof of the pudding" that one is honestly aiming to be accountable for bad decisions and actions. It typically needs to happen before other possible healing actions, such as forgiveness and reconciliation, are possible.

Unfortunately however, abusers may engage in an inappropriate form of confession in an effort to feel or think better about themselves, to cope with their situation, to further control their partner, or induce her to forgive and forget. This may seem to have happened in the parable of the Prodigal Son, where the father who had been hurt responded with incredible grace and welcomed the son home, no questions asked.

Grace is the unmerited favor of God toward man, or of one person toward another. Unsolicited grace is a key teaching of the Christian religion. However, as theologian Dietrich Bonhoeffer has noted, claims of confession in an effort to gain a favor, or get something for nothing, amount to seeking "cheap grace." An abuser who doesn't really change, but confesses in order to manipulate his partner to do what he wants, is looking for cheap grace. Instead, Bonhoeffer has said that confession should be "the God-given remedy for self-deception and self-indulgence," enabling Christians to unlearn their sinful ways through communion with God and one another.[7]

Thus, the purpose of confession to self, God, or another person is not to get something you want or need when things aren't going your way. In fact, victims of abuse may, for many valid reasons, respond negatively or not at all to even a sincere confession. Instead, the purpose of your confession is to help you deal with your self-deception and self-indulgence, and move you forward on your journey toward transforming your life, while helping your victim with her own healing journey. You need to start the process by confessing to yourself and to God.

Confess to Self

People are often dishonest with themselves. As discussed in earlier chapters, they often minimize, justify, deny, rationalize, and blame to avoid facing up to what they have done and their responsibility for the consequences of their behavior. Hiding from ourselves in these ways keeps us broken, fearful, and at some level both arrogant and afraid of ourselves at the same time. It makes us dishonest, and therefore unable to deal honestly with others.

Confessing your abusive behavior or other misdeeds to yourself is a way of being honest in dealing with what you have done and affirming that you have accepted responsibility and are accountable.

Confessing to yourself is honestly answering to that small inner voice, that inborn feeling that helps you decide between right and wrong, called the conscience. When you answer to your conscience, you face up to your situation and move toward being accountable to God and others.

You can confess to yourself in either or all of several ways.

Think in Solitude

Solitude is when you are alone, but you are not lonely. You are comfortable with your own company. Solitude is not a time to just get out of the house, escape the challenges of the day, or use your absence to punish your partner or family. Instead, it is your personal time for reflection, inner searching, or talking to yourself about your past and your future. Healthy solitude—not escaping or running away, which could be a form of abuse—gives you the time and privacy to gain perspective on your life, and to think deeply about how you have been abusive and what you should do about it.

Confessing to yourself by thinking in solitude is your way of privately acknowledging your behavior and making plans to deal with it. You can create an opportunity for personal reflection by taking a long walk or run, spending some private time in your favorite place, or going fishing by yourself. Talk to yourself about what you have done and your need to confess.

Confess to a Third Party

Chapter 2 discussed dialogue, a conversation in which two or more people exchange information, ideas, opinions, or feelings; and from which you can gain new insights and understandings, and learn more about yourself. Confidential dialogue with someone not involved in your abuse—a minister, counselor, friend, or even stranger—can provide you an opportunity to "privately" talk about issues of concern or acknowledge your behavior and make plans to deal with it, but with someone to stimulate your thinking and provide critical feedback. Such confessing to a dis-interested party can be a way of confessing to yourself and setting the stage for confessing to God and the victim of your abuse.

But remember, as discussed above, the purpose of such a discussion, like your confession, is to address your own self-deception and self-indulgence," and unlearn your abusive habits. So, don't try to gain favor, or "cheap grace," by blaming your partner, or minimizing, justifying, or denying your abuse, or by claiming credit for seeking help to change.

Pray

The next section discusses confessing to God. Confessing to Him in prayer requires preparation. You can't ask for something until you know what to acknowledge or ask for. Thus, you have to think about yourself and assess your own faults and needs, including your need for God's help and blessing, before you pray. This preparation and prayer is another way of confessing to yourself.

Write in a Journal

Keeping a journal can be a form of confession in solitude, where you open your heart through writing about yourself. By writing in a journal, you can confess secrets, emotions, pain, and shame that you do not yet feel you can share with anyone. You can surrender yourself with the certain knowledge that you will never be rejected, scolded, reprimanded, or betrayed. Since only you and God know what you are writing, you can know that you will be accepted and loved.

Write a Letter and Don't Send It

Unsent letters, a form of journal, can be very effective because thinking of a specific recipient and how you may have offended them helps you be more specific in your confession to yourself. If you write a letter honestly confessing to your partner and don't send it, you are confessing to yourself.

Confess to God

An honest relationship with God is impossible if you deny your faults and don't come clean with Him. The Bible teaches that you need to confess your wrongs to receive God's life within you. Confession practices vary widely, of course, from the more formal, confidential Sacrament of Penance in the Roman Catholic Church to less formal, sometimes more public confessions of other Christian traditions. It is a foundation of Christian teaching, however, that confession is necessary for a person to transform his life.

To help you think in general terms about how you should confess to God, let's continue with the story of David, introduced in the discussion on responsibility in Chapter 5. David was truly sorry for his adultery with Bathsheba, for murdering her husband to cover it up, and for his other sins. Psalm 51:1–6 tells of his confession to God:

> Have mercy on me, O God, according to your unfailing love; according to your great compassion blot out my transgressions. Wash away all my iniquity and cleanse me from my sin. For I know my transgressions, and my sin is always before me. Against you, you only, have I sinned and done what is evil in your sight; so you are right in your verdict and justified when you judge. Surely I was sinful at birth, sinful from the time my mother conceived me. Yet you desired faithfulness even in the womb; you taught me wisdom in that secret place.

David reflected on his confession, and the joy of God's forgiveness for his sins against Bathsheba and Uriah, in Psalm 32:3–5:

> When I kept silent, my bones wasted away through my groaning all day long. For day and night your hand was heavy on me; my strength was sapped as in the heat of summer. Then I acknowledged my sin to you and did not cover up my iniquity. I said, "I will confess my transgressions to the Lord." And you forgave the guilt of my sin.

Confess to God in your own special way, according to the dictates of your religious tradition. Using David as a model will be helpful. You can pray to God and acknowledge what you've done. Confessing to yourself and to God will usually help improve your relationship with others. This may—or may not—suggest you should confess to your partner, which will be discussed in the following chapter.

Questions for Reflection or Group Study

1. What is the most important lesson you learned about confession from the story of the Prodigal Son?

2. Was the son's confession to his father an example of seeking cheap grace? Explain your answer.

3. What is the most important lesson you learned about confession from Psalm 51 and Psalm 32?

4. What does confessing to yourself mean? How should you go about it?

5. Considering your own religious beliefs, how should you confess to your God?

6. List several examples of what you probably should confess to yourself and to God.

7. How does confessing to yourself and God help prepare you to confess to a person you have hurt?

> ### Personal Reflection
>
> Which of the learning objectives for this chapter is most important to you in stopping abuse and transforming your life? Why?

CHAPTER 10

Confession to Others

> ### Learning Objectives
>
> After completing this chapter, you should be able to:
> - Decide whether and when confessing to an abused partner is appropriate.
> - Confess to your partner in a way that demonstrates your honesty, sincerity, and humility.
> - Respect that your partner may be fearful or unwilling to hear a confession.
> - Determine what process is best for confessing if appropriate in your situation.

IN AN HONEST CONFESSION, YOU ACCEPT REsponsibility for what you have done, acknowledge your accountability to the one(s) you have hurt, turn from your abusive behavior, and reform your life. As discussed in Chapter 9, confession is not cheap grace, but instead is a clear acknowledgment of your accountability to self and to God, and an honest commitment to change.

Confession to people you have hurt or abused is like an apology, and confessing what you have done often is very important to stopping abuse and transforming your life. However, sometimes confessing a wrongdoing may be ill-advised, as discussed next. Further, confessing to a partner you have abused may not be feasible or appropriate, as she may not feel safe or comfortable enough to hear what you have to say.

As discussed in Chapter 9, the purpose of confession is not to get something you want or need, or to convince your partner you understand her needs. Instead, it is to help you deal with your self-deception and self-indulgence, and move you forward on your journey toward transforming your life, while also helping your partner on her healing journey.

Therefore, you need to think seriously about whether to confess, when to do so, and how you should go about it.

Decide Whether to Confess

Confession is a choice. Your decision whether to confess may be influenced by what you have done and which of two purposes is present.

Decide Whether to Confess to Something the Other Person Doesn't Know

If your partner doesn't know about an indiscretion or something bad you have been involved in, it may or may not be best for you to confess. Where you have secretly violated the respect, trust, or rights of your partner—for example, if you have had a secret affair—confession can be "like opening a boil." You need to be sure everyone is ready before you do so. Sometimes you need to open a boil so it will heal and the hurting will stop, and sometimes you need to confess to secret matters to prevent hurt to your partner if you don't. But at other times, a confession will make your problem worse and lead to long-term hurt of the other person. Don't confess to something the other person isn't aware of if you honestly believe there are no compelling reasons to do so and doing so will hurt them for the long-term—and actually be another form of abuse. You have to decide, and the question often is complex enough that professional advice should be obtained. Accordingly, the following comments address confessing your abusive behavior that directly affects your partner, and that she is aware of.

Confess Your Abuse

You, and your partner, know that certain of your behavior has been abusive, inappropriate, or hurtful. Honestly and sincerely confessing and being accountable to her for such obvious abuse—the yelling, the threats, the violence—is nearly always appropriate if she is willing and able to engage with you.

But domestic abuse is also about controlling someone's mind and emotions, and sometimes it is less obvious: a putdown here or there, a bad excuse to keep her away from family or friends, questionable accusations and blame, unfair criticism, and such. Confessing such behavior and discussing it may be an excellent way of starting to deal with it. However, sometimes confessing in such confusing situations is like opening a boil, and doing so may be questionable. A great guide in deciding whether to confess is to use the phrase from the Hippocratic Oath that governs ethics of the medical profession: "to abstain from doing harm." If confessing will likely do harm, it probably should not be done. You may want to take a pass for the time being.

A confession most likely will do no harm if it is honest, respects your partner's boundaries and feelings, and is true to God, yourself, and others in genuinely accepting responsibility for what you have done, acknowledging your accountability, and being committed to turn from your misdeeds and reform your life and your relationship with the other person. Confessing to one you have hurt puts your offending behavior to the front and demonstrates your feelings and your honesty. It helps you deal with your self-deception and self-indulgence. And hopefully, telling the difficult, shameful, risky truth will begin to build trust in the other person and provide some evidence that she can depend on you in the future.

Honestly confessing your abusive actions to the one you have hurt is usually difficult and often takes real courage. It's easy to think of wrong reasons for not confessing. You probably are ashamed of your behavior, and your shame is made worse when you talk about what you have done. Your pride holds you back, as you don't want your accomplishments diminished by confession of your abuse. You wonder whether acknowledging your mistakes isn't a sign of weakness rather than a sign of strength. Minimizing, justifying, denying, blaming, and rationalizing are much easier. Saying, "I was wrong, and I am sorry," takes guts. If considerations such as these are preventing you from confessing to your partner, you need to deal with them.

Should you always confess—apologize for—your abusive behavior? Probably so, if you can confess honestly and sincerely. However, a dishonest, insincere confession will do more harm than good. It will deceive both you and your partner. It will slow her healing journey. It will put you deeper in the hole of your own faults and shame. Rather than freeing the two of you, it will entrap you. Rather than confirming your honesty, morality, and strength, a dishonest confession will lead to or reinforce a cycle of lying, hypocrisy, and weakness. Your partner will become more cynical about you, less trusting of you. Rather than improving your relationship, an insincere confession will speed its decline.

On the other hand, if you have genuinely accepted responsibility for what you have done, and are committed to turning from your misdeeds and reforming your life, acknowledging your accountability through confession is nearly always appropriate.

Decide When to Confess

When is the right time to confess? You can confess to yourself and to God whenever the spirit moves you, but confessing to one you have hurt can sometimes be a difficult decision. However, if you want to make things right, you will probably have to make the first move when you believe the time is as good as it is likely to get. Knowing when to bring up the past, and when not to, requires an insight and understanding of yourself and your partner. Confessing at the right time—when both you and the one to whom you are confessing are ready—helps you choose the right words and tone and improves your ability to listen to your partner's response. Consider the following:

- Are you ready? Be sure to understand enough about your situation to raise the issues you need to raise and the other person needs to hear, and to communicate in detail about your behavior and its consequences. As discussed above, be sure you have taken responsibility for your actions and can apologize honestly. Be sure you have confessed to God and to yourself before confessing to your partner. And be as sure as possible that your confession will do no harm.

- Is your partner ready? Try to decide whether your partner is able and willing to allow you to apologize. Is she too fearful to hear what you will say? Does she have too little trust in you? Has your behavior been so bad that even listening to a confession would trivialize what you have done? Consider the possibility that your partner can't honestly accept a confession at the time, and that your confession will actually hurt your relationship. Proceed only when you believe your partner is ready and willing to hear what you say.

Sometimes it may be helpful to confess first to a third person. Part of the value of confession is being listened to, and a neutral person is often a better listener than someone who is directly involved. You may need someone to listen to your confession without any personal interest and without agreeing or disagreeing with you. You may have wise friends who are willing to listen and hold you accountable; or you may need to find a pastor, counselor, psychologist, or other appropriate professional. Just telling your story to a good listener helps you see things as they are and can be a dress rehearsal for your confession to someone you have hurt.

Sometimes you need to consider whether you can sincerely confess, or whether you should spare both of you from aggravation and move on. If you are not sure, however, err on the side of confessing when you can do so honestly, without hurting your partner. Honestly confessing will help you see yourself as you are, and can be a good first step toward your transformation.

A borrowed story says a great deal about confession and how to confess: "A man said in confession, 'Father, I stole a rope.' He neglected to say that there was a cow at the end of the rope!" Unlike this man's claimed confession, real confession requires honesty, enough detail to convey the complete truth, and a penitent spirit. The story sets the stage for the following section.

Decide How to Confess

If you have accepted responsibility and are accountable for your abusive behavior, you have made a good start toward stopping it and changing your life. Now consider confessing to further your own change and help your victim heal. Confess first to yourself and affirm your responsibility. Take full responsibility and be fully accountable to the other person. Don't try to deny or justify what you have done. Do not shift blame or assign excuses, as this will only begin a negative cycle and make matters worse. There very rarely is a place for the word "but" in a confession. You need to just tell the truth. Some thoughts for doing this are as follows.

Be Specific Without Overdoing the Details

You may have physically hurt your partner, embarrassed her, prevented her from realizing her full potential, or committed other hurtful acts against her. The past cannot be changed, but simply saying a blanket "I'm sorry" will do little to restore the trust and potential that formerly existed.

Trying to confess with generalities and trite remarks seems insincere and leaves the other person to wonder whether you really understand what you are doing or are being honest about it. Generalities and often-used comments build cynicism rather than trust, push apart rather than bring together, hurt rather than heal. Confessions need to be specific enough that it's clear you are taking responsibility for your past actions. For example:

- I tried to manipulate you when I _____ .

- I lied to you when I _____ .

- I hurt you in so many ways when I hit you last Saturday night.

- I am sorry because I love you and realize and acknowledge how my attempts to control you, like the time I _____, have hurt you.

You can accept responsibility and confess without discussing all the gory details or reopening old wounds. Think about your confession in advance, aim to do no harm, and respond to the reactions of your partner. Be straightforward and simple, without overdoing the details or becoming overly dramatic. Use language that acknowledges your guilt and doesn't shift the blame to your partner

Demonstrate Humility

If you approach a situation with arrogance, or let your pride show, your confession will not work. What is it like to be humble? Paul tells us in Philippians 2:3–7:

> Do nothing out of selfish ambition or vain conceit. Rather, in humility value others above yourselves, not looking to your own interests but each of you to the interests of the others. In your relationships with one another, have the same mindset as Christ Jesus: Who, being in very nature God, did not consider equality

with God something to be used to his own advantage; rather, he made himself nothing by taking the very nature of a servant, being made in human likeness.

Humility is having a modest opinion of one's own importance or rank; being meek; not having a false pride. It envisions a belief that we, men and women, are all equal human beings in the sight of God. It's the opposite of trying to dominate or control someone else. It leads us to do what we can to benefit others.

Paul's lesson to "Do nothing out of selfish ambition or vain conceit. Rather, in humility value others above yourselves," no doubt applies equally to both men and women. But that's the point! Equal treatment suggests that neither is dominant over the other. If a man expects or demands a woman to be humble toward him, he is exhibiting the worst form of arrogance, hubris, and hypocrisy. Humility and equality need to focus on the individual's (man or woman) own spiritual development, and demands for them should not be used to manipulate or abuse another.

Show Respect

Honor the person to whom you are confessing. Respect involves how you see the other person rather than how you show yourself. Respect means treating your partner as you would want to be treated. It involves believing she will receive a confession, perhaps asking permission before proceeding, acknowledging her humanity and the fact that she has a right to feel hurt. Confessing with respect acknowledges both what you did and how you affected her.

Be Honest with Your Emotions

True confession is an emotional experience, both for you and the other person. Confession usually involves guilt, shame, fear, uncertainty, pride, pain, and other feelings. Don't deny this fact or try to hide it. Let your honest emotions show without being antagonistic or threatening, and accept those of the person you are confessing to. If you don't honestly feel any emotions, don't try to manufacture them.

Use Whatever Communication Approach Fits Best

Abusers will not always be able to confess to a partner or former partner. Their partners may not feel safe or trust that they have changed. The victim's pain may just be too great.

However if confessing is appropriate and safe, in most cases nothing is better than a face-to-face verbal confession, where the emotion can be felt, the tears observed, the person hugged. However, such contact may not be appropriate if you cannot control your anger or other emotions; and it may not be feasible, as it may be prevented by the victim's continuing fear, a court order, or other circumstances. In such cases, a letter, phone call, or email may be more appropriate or perhaps necessary, provided your victim is not afraid, and is willing to share her address and receive your correspondence.

Further, confessing by mail will sometimes be more effective than other choices. Doing so if okay with your partner gives you time to choose your words carefully, and it gives the person to whom you are confessing time to reflect, think about your confession, and perhaps pray about whether and how to respond or whether not to respond at all.

As is often the case, you need to think about the situation and do what you believe is most respectful of the person you've harmed.

CONFESSION TO OTHERS

Questions for Reflection or Group Study

1. How should you deal with those who have hurt you and should confess to you but have chosen not to?

2. Provide an example of when you abused someone. List the people to whom you should consider confessing for this abuse.

3. In the example cited, would confessing now be the right thing, or would it do more harm than good? What factors affect your opinion?

4. List some reasons your partner might not accept a confession from you?

5. How should you handle a situation where you would like to confess to your partner but she is not likely to be willing to accept a confession?

6. What do you think is usually the best way to confess?

CONFESSION TO OTHERS

7. How do you think you and your partner would feel if you confessed your abuse to her?

> ## Personal Reflection
>
> Which of the learning objectives for this chapter is most important to you in stopping abuse and transforming your life? Why?

CHAPTER 11
God's Forgiveness

Learning Objectives

After completing this chapter, you should be able to:
- Explain that forgiveness is the granting of free pardon or giving up resentment for a hurt or debt against us, and does not condone, justify, or excuse abusive or coercive behavior.
- See forgiveness as a journey that helps get you beyond childhood traumas and past hurts.
- Ask for God's forgiveness with the confident expectation that you will receive it, and that it will benefit your mind, body, and soul.
- Forgive yourself and get beyond self-hatred, without in any way condoning, excusing, or justifying abuse.

MANASSEH BECAME KING OF JUDAH WHEN HE was only twelve years old and reigned for fifty-five years as one of the most evil of all kings. Among his many evils, he sacrificed his own children as burnt offerings, and tradition has it that he probably gave the order to have Isaiah the prophet sawn in two. He encouraged every sort of evil, and even seduced Judah and the inhabitants of Jerusalem to do more evil. He was a bad man, and he made God very angry.

After Manasseh was defeated in battle and taken prisoner he cried out to God for help, humbling himself and asking for mercy and grace. "And the Lord listened, and answered his plea by returning him to Jerusalem and to his kingdom! At that point Manasseh finally realized that the Lord was really God." (2 Chronicles 33: 1–13) Manasseh, a sinful man who did many evil things, asked for forgiveness and God forgave him.

Similarly, forgiveness is available for you—even if you have separated from your partner or other loved ones, are on probation or otherwise subject to requirements of the judicial system, or perhaps are or have been in jail or prison because of your abusive behavior. But being forgiven does not mean what you did will be forgotten or was okay or justifiable, or that you are free to do it again. So—what does forgiveness mean for you?

About Forgiveness

Forgiving a person is granting free pardon or giving up resentment for a hurt or debt that person brought against us. It involves looking back at what happened but not for the purpose of analyzing, blaming, or condemning. Forgiveness looks back for the purpose of leaving the offense behind and moving on to a better future. Forgiveness does not change the past or the abuse that happened, but it does change the present and can change the future.

Forgiveness Is

Forgiveness—both forgiving another and being forgiven—is a matter of the heart, the inner self, that involves a change in internal feeling as well as a change in external action. Forgiveness can lead to a way of life that is focused on addressing brokenness and experiencing peace in the present moment.

Forgiveness fosters a feeling of peace, as it helps people take hurt less personally and take responsibility for how they feel, without in any way accepting or condoning the actions against them.

Being forgiven does not condone your abuse, but it can help you transform your life by facing and dealing with the guilt and shame of your abusive behavior. It also sets the stage for communion with God and, to the extent feasible as discussed in Chapter 14, pursuing a form of communion with your victim.

Studies have shown that forgiveness is beneficial to one's health. Anger, blame, holding grudges, guilt, and shame are seen as contributing to cardiovascular problems. Dealing with such hurtful emotions by forgiving or being forgiven leads to improvements in the cardiovascular and nervous systems. Forgiveness increases one's positive emotions and feelings of hope, care, affection, trust, and happiness, and helps develop an enhanced spiritual view, all of which contribute to physical health and improve the ability to deal with pain.[8]

Forgiveness Is Not

Let's now look at what forgiveness is not if you have abused a woman:

- Forgiving is not an obligation of your victim, and you should not expect her forgiveness. Your belief that forgiveness would benefit you is not a legitimate basis for insisting on forgiveness. Instead, a person who has been abused may choose whether or not to forgive her abuser—and may decide not to do so for good and legitimate reasons, or for no reason at all. Whether or not forgiveness is offered, you still have the responsibility to stop your abuse, change, and grow.

- Forgiving or being forgiven does not condone abusive behavior, justify it, or make it okay. When someone forgives you, they are not saying your abuse was right or acceptable to them.

- Forgiving does not mean forgetting. It is getting beyond, not forgetting, denying, or minimizing. A person can forgive while still remembering in great detail what happened, and even while experiencing its impact. For example, a victim may deal with a long-term injury or disability, have a traumatic brain injury, have trauma responses or even grieve the death of a loved one at the hands of the person who perpetrated violence—and still seek to forgive.

- Forgiving does not equate to mercy, do away with the consequences for the abuser, or suggest that justice is not appropriate. A person who hurts another cannot ignore the consequences. Even if forgiven, he has to face the consequences, whether the natural consequences directly or indirectly flowing from his action (like his wife continuing to insist on a divorce), or those imposed by the legal system (like going to jail).

- Forgiveness does not justify continuing abuse. Abuse, even if forgiven by God or the victim, is always a violation of Gods law and human rights, and often of state law.

- Forgiving does not mean establishing a close relationship. It allows you to get on with your life, with or without the other person. Whether you should have a relationship, and if so what kind, should stand on its own merits.

Forgiveness is a key element in your journey to stop abuse, transform your life, and restore peace in your life and the lives of your loved ones. This chapter will discuss God's forgiveness, and explore the question of "forgiving yourself." Chapter 12 will focus on forgiving others and being forgiven by them.

God's Forgiveness

God forgave Manasseh, and He is willing to forgive you for your wrongs—even for the abuse you have heaped on others. You are made in God's image, He loves you, and you are not beyond His forgiveness. The Apostle Paul wrote in Romans 3:23–24, "for all have sinned and fall short of the glory of God, and all are justified freely by his grace . . ."

Remember, however, that God's forgiveness is not cheap grace, but a process in which you need to do several things as well.

- First, you need to be remorseful for what you have done and for your abuse of others.

- Second, you should have mercy on your fellow human beings and those who have hurt you, such as a father who abused you or a business partner who cheated you. "For if you forgive other people when they sin against you, your heavenly Father will also forgive you. But if you do not forgive others their sins, your Father will not forgive your sins." (Matthew 6:14–15)

- Third, forgiveness demands confession, repentance, and love of others—all discussed in previous chapters.

- Finally, you need to seek forgiveness from God and your fellow human beings on a continuing, ongoing basis.

Thus, God's forgiveness is available to you. It doesn't justify causing harm or mean it is okay to abuse others. Instead, it can help you grow spiritually and transform your life. Your challenge is to forgive those who have hurt you, accept God's forgiveness, and change your life.

Forgiving Yourself

John was thirty-five and Shirley was twenty-three when they met. After a fun courtship, marred only occasionally by some disagreements when John tried to tell Shirley what to do, they got married. Life was great for a while, and then problems began to occur. John would gripe about the dirty dishes or unmade bed, or make comments like: "Are you going to wear that outfit? That's not very attractive on you." Then it progressed to: "You're ugly," or "You're stupid," and "No one else is going to want to be with you."

Over the years John's behavior became more controlling and emotionally abusive. His verbal assaults turned physical, and he would yell, push, and throw things in Shirley's direction. Sometimes he would push her to the ground and actually hit her. The hitting became beating, first occasionally and then almost every day. Even when Shirley was pregnant, John did not care. When Shirley told John she was planning to leave, he threw threats around and used the children as pawns. He said he would sue her for full custody, and would prove she wasn't a fit mother because she had gone to therapy. John told Shirley that if she left him, she would be forfeiting her right to their property, and he'd take everything.

Shirley often had black eyes, busted lips, and a bruised body. She had a broken heart too. After the worst incidents, John would often cry, ask for forgiveness, and promise to never abuse her again. And then the next day he returned to the worst.

One night Shirley went out with friends, and when she got home John yelled and screamed at her for being out too late. She told him he needed to leave, and he hit her across the face a couple of times. When Shirley ran for her phone to call for help, John grabbed it and crushed it with the heel of his boot. He kept saying, "why are you making me do this?" as he grabbed her hair, dragged her into the bedroom, slammed the door, and beat her almost beyond recognition.

After that last incident of abuse, the judge in charge of John's case got his attention. The more John reflects on his behavior, the guiltier he feels. He knows he is responsible for what he has done, and sometimes shame and remorse seem to overtake him. He would genuinely like to put abuse behind and change his life.

John wants Shirley's forgiveness and love, but his guilt and shame tear him apart when he remembers the pain in her eyes and thinks about how badly he hurt her. John realizes he is not entitled to Shirley's love or forgiveness, and she may not be willing to grant it. But God's forgiveness and his own forgiveness are available to him. He wants to forgive himself, because he believes he cannot change his life unless he does. But doing so seems hypocritical, as he feels he has been a monster in so many ways. He would like to be forgiven for what he has done, but he wonders how this is possible when he can't even forgive himself. John needs to do two things.

Aceept God's Forgiveness

Can John forgive himself? Does anyone have the right or authority to forgive himself for hurting others? Looking at how God is willing to forgive us is a way to consider this question.

God forgave Manasseh, even with all his evil deeds, and He surely will forgive you when you have done wrong. We are all sinners. We often are unable to see ourselves in that light, but we are part of the human condition in which we are neither angels nor monsters. Human beings have great capacity for evil, and some work very hard at becoming sinners, but we are made in God's image, He loves us, and no one is beyond His forgiveness.

Thus God's forgiveness is available to all of us, and with His willingness to forgive it seems the rest should be easy. It isn't, however, so let's move to forgiving yourself.

Forgive Self

It seems to John that forgiving himself for his failures and all the hurt he has caused to Shirley, their children, families, and others is the same as saying what he did was okay, and he knows it wasn't. Feeling guilty and ashamed feels better than feeling forgiven, so he is trapped in his own guilt and shame over what he did in the past. Since he cannot forgive himself, John feels paralyzed and unable to get beyond his past to a better future. Instead, he is stuck "hoping for a better past."

Reasonable people might disagree whether you can forgive yourself. But God will forgive you, and you can accept God's grace and His forgiveness after you have confessed and repented to yourself and to God.

Unless your standards are higher than God's, you can forgive yourself.

Forgiving yourself is embracing God, accepting his forgiveness, and walking with him. It means getting beyond the self-hatred that goes along with not forgiving yourself, and owning what you have done, while not being defined by your worst or best moments. It means not trying to escape or numb your shame through negative behavior such as drinking or using drugs, stopping punishing yourself, setting yourself free to change your life, and committing to changing your life for the better. It means accepting God's blessings and grace.

Importantly, forgiving yourself does not condone or excuse what you have done, and it does not justify abuse in the future. Abuse of anyone is always unacceptable to God and man, and forgiveness does not make it acceptable. Further, forgiving yourself is a journey rather than a onetime event, and it carries with it a commitment to change your behavior and your life. Forgiving yourself without changing your unacceptable behavior is a sign of nothing more than moral shallowness.

We've discussed the first part. God has promised His forgiveness, and you can "forgive yourself" by accepting His forgiveness. But forgiving one another is often much more difficult. This will be discussed in the following chapter.

Questions for Reflection or Group Study

1. What are the most important lessons for you from the actions of Manasseh and the actions of God in the story of 2 Chronicles 33:1–13?

   Manasseh:

   God:

2. Why is God's forgiveness important for you?

3. What should you do if you want God to forgive you?

4. What does it mean to "forgive yourself?"

5. Why should you forgive yourself for your abusive behavior?

6. What does forgiving yourself not mean in abusive situations?

Personal Reflection

Which of the learning objectives for this chapter is most important to you in stopping abuse and transforming your life? Why?

CHAPTER 12
Practicing Forgiveness

Learning Objectives

After completing this chapter, you should be able to:
- Discuss several important characteristics of forgiving and asking for forgiveness.
- Identify any persons in your life whom you need to forgive, and take appropriate action, particularly emphasizing those who may have mistreated you as a child.
- Discern whether you should ask a person you have abused for forgiveness, and do so if appropriate.
- React responsibly if a person chooses not to forgive you.

Let's start this chapter by revisiting parts of the Chapter 11 discussion of what forgiveness is and is not: Forgiving or being forgiven is granting free pardon or giving up resentment for a hurt or debt against the person doing the forgiving. Forgiveness does not condone abusive behavior, justify it, or make it okay. Forgiving is not an obligation of the victim, and being forgiven should not be an expectation of the abuser.

More About Forgiveness

Forgiveness cuts both ways. Sometimes an abuser needs to ask for forgiveness for things he has done, and sometimes he needs to grant it to those who have hurt him. Either way, it should never be used to try to minimize an abuser's bad behavior or to manipulate or blame the victim. Instead, forgiveness should become a way of life that begins to clear the deck, and hopefully helps you stop your abuse and violence and move toward transforming your life, while also helping the victim gain a measure of peace.

No one can force another person to forgive, ask for forgiveness, or accept forgiveness, and no one can prevent others from forgiving. Each person has to decide what they will do in a particular situation. Certain characteristics of forgiveness apply to both forgiving and asking for forgiveness. You should apply the following when facing a possible forgiveness situation.

Forgive Unconditionally

When you choose to forgive someone, your forgiveness should be unconditional, not dependent on the actions of the person who did the harm or their admission of guilt or wrongdoing. If someone has hurt you, you can welcome their confession and repentance if it occurs, and even create a climate that encourages it. But you cannot force another person to do what you think they should do. They will act as they wish.

If you should consider forgiving another person, but require them to do something before you are willing to forgive, you are: (1) giving that person the power to control whether and when you forgive. You are allowing a double hurt, once in the original offense and the second when the other person refuses to do what you want; and (2) you are probably using your prerequisite for forgiveness as a means for further controlling and abusing the other person. You are trying to get them to do something they don't want to do—a key aspect of abuse.

Thus, to prevent the other person from being in control and hurting you again, and avoid further abusing them, you need to forgive unconditionally. Don't make your forgiveness dependent on their actions.

Forgive When It Is Difficult

Forgiveness can be very difficult, as we often feel so badly hurt that our pride tends to prevent us from giving a break to the person who hurt us, or we may feel that forgiveness tends to condone the offending action.

Forgiving another person can be easier if you really think deeply about what happened and put it all in the proper context. Remember that forgiving is not condoning or justifying the other person's bad actions. It is getting beyond them. Further, considering all the facts and being open to understanding the intent of the person who hurt you. often leads to a conclusion that the offense was not as bad as you thought. You may start out believing their intent was motivated by malice, but come to understand that they didn't intend to cause you harm. If you remind yourself that you are just one among many who have suffered such an offense, it may seem less significant. You probably are not the first, and you will not be the last. Remember that in many cases the person did not intend to hurt you personally. Refusing to see an offense as a personal attack makes forgiving it easier.

Forgiving is also difficult for others, particularly for victims of abuse. Sometimes the abuse has been so bad, things have gone so far, that forgiveness would seem to trivialize the abuse, and is not morally justified. Or the victim may fear that the forgiveness will be misinterpreted by the perpetrator and cause him to continue the abuse, and therefore refuse to forgive for good reason.

Forgive In Your Heart

Forgiveness is an internal decision of the heart, so the person doing the forgiving doesn't necessarily have to confront the person being forgiven. The person being forgiven may or may not even know they have been forgiven. Forgiveness does not demand that you communicate with the other person. It often is mainly for you and may take place, for example, after the person being forgiven is out of the picture.

Sometimes telling another you forgive them might be construed as arrogant and too judgmental, and the person will resent it rather than accept it. You may need, for your own reasons, to forgive someone for something he does not believe was wrong, for which he does not want forgiveness, or that he isn't even aware of. In such cases, communicating forgiveness is a form of accusation that may lay a guilt trip on the other person and not be helpful. You are not the judge, and you don't have to confront to forgive.

However, telling someone you forgive them is often a powerful blessing to both of you. In deciding, you should always remember the earlier advice in a different context: do no harm. In particularly difficult situations, consider discussing the question with a counselor or minister.

Continue Forgiving

We need to keep on forgiving and lead a forgiving life. When Jesus was asked how many times we should forgive, He answered "seventy times seven," which seems to mean there is no end to our need to forgive. (Matthew 18:22) We need to unlearn our habits of anger, hate, and vindictiveness, and learn to live as a forgiven and forgiving person.

Forgiving Others

All of us probably have occasion to forgive others. For our purpose here, let's consider two situations where you, as an abuser, may need to be the one doing the forgiving.

- Forgiving those who you have hurt: When you related your story in Chapter 2, did you identify any people who have hurt you? Are you still carrying pain or grudges caused by them? You may have been abused, exposed to abuse in your family, or hurt by others in various ways. You may have feelings of resentment, anger, and vindictiveness toward them. Are these feelings making it more difficult for you to change your life? Probably so, which means you need to consider forgiving them.

- In an abusive situation, the question usually is whether the victim will forgive you. However, on occasion a victim of abuse may do things for which forgiveness by a person who has been abusing her needs to be considered. For example, your partner may do things that cause you pain because she is responding to your abuse, trying to escape your abuse, or possibly for other reasons. Deciding to forgive your partner for the pain you experience will help you to let go of resentment and choose to respond with compassion, respect and nonviolence. You should carefully consider granting forgiveness in such a situation. Failing to reasonably forgive a partner, or using the situation to manipulate or further hurt her, is itself a form of abuse.

Forgiving those who have hurt you, past or present, seems perfectly consistent with God's plan that we forgive in order to be forgiven. In addition to giving the forgiven person a measure of relief, you will benefit immeasurably from forgiving those who hurt you. Doing so will help free you from the negative effects of your anger, minimize any tendency you may have toward vengeance or vindictiveness, provide greater spiritual and psychological well-being, reduce anxiety and stress, and set the stage for transforming your life.

Being Forgiven

We want to be forgiven for our offenses and for hurting another if we are truly remorseful. Being forgiven shows us that there is sufficient goodness in us that someone else has judged us forgivable and allowed us to begin to find our peace. It helps us release our conscience from the guilt and shame we are carrying around, and it can help mend a broken or estranged relationship.

Chapter 11 introduced John and Shirley, and discussed John's abuse and his need to receive God's forgiveness and to "forgive himself." John would genuinely like to put abuse behind and change his life, and he also feels a need to be forgiven by those he has hurt, particularly by Shirley. But he isn't sure whether he deserves her forgiveness. And he is concerned that her forgiveness is not possible because she is afraid of him and does not trust that he will stop the abuse.

John has created a situation where Shirley is filled with mistrust, anger, fear, even hatred at times. In the past John would often cry, ask for forgiveness, and promise to never abuse her again. And then the next day he would continue the worst of the abuse. Aren't Shirley's feelings of anger and mistrust morally justified under the circumstances? Why should she forgive him when John seems to take it as minimizing the significance of the abuse, even making the abuse seem okay and giving him permission to continue with it? Why should she forgive him when history suggests John's abuse will continue or get worse if she does?

Trying to force another person to forgive you is more likely to lead to lying and further degradation of your relationship than to moral and spiritual rebirth. Whether or not Shirley is willing to forgive John will depend on many factors, most of which John can control: whether he demonstrates love and respect toward her, whether he honestly is trying to change, whether he does things that make her afraid of him, and other such considerations. Another somewhat different consideration involves the question of reconciliation and a whether they have a future together.

Forgiveness Without Reconciliation

Sometimes forgiveness is a little like individual counseling that focuses on a person who has been hurt and involves her ability to cope with her feelings. It involves a victim forgiving an abuser who has hurt her in order to get beyond the anger and hatred felt toward the abuser, and hopefully to help her find peace. In the case of John and Shirley it would involve Shirley forgiving John, perhaps telling him she forgives him, both of them feeling better as a result, and moving on (perhaps after a divorce) with her life as a "clean slate," separate from John.

While not necessarily easy, this level of forgiveness is feasible in most situations. It may help the parties achieve a level of peace that would not exist without forgiveness.

Forgiveness With Reconciliation

At another level, forgiveness involves more than a word spoken, an action taken, a feeling felt, or simply moving beyond anger and hatred. Instead, forgiveness in this context includes some form of reconciliation and restoration of communion between the people involved. Such reconciliation, discussed in more detail in Chapter 14, does not have to mean that they maintain their intimate partner relationship. It could involve various types of relationships, from co-parenting, to working together, to recognizing separate assets and such, that include a restoration of communion between the people involved. This level of forgiveness might involve Shirley forgiving John and continuing some meaningful relationship with him, with John obligated to stop the abuse and change his life.

Reconciliation, even when forgiveness is present, may or may not be possible or appropriate in many cases of abuse. Those involved may need to seek appropriate, individual professional counseling to assist in making a decision.

Asking for Forgiveness

If you have, like John, dominated and abused a partner, and created a high level of anger, fear, and distrust in her, what do you need to do if you want her forgiveness—and probably the forgiveness of others you have hurt as well?

Remember that forgiving you is the other person's choice. There is no way you can coerce it. They may be unable, at least at the time, to move beyond the fear, anger, resentment, and personal hurt and loss caused by your abuse. They may feel that forgiving you compromises their sense of safety and self-respect. They may believe that forgiveness requires them to make a moral compromise. Regardless of whether you agree with such attitudes, if they hold them they are theirs, and those attitudes will determine whether and when they will forgive you.

Asking for forgiveness is asking someone to do something important for you. You need to ask with humility and respect. Would you ask for another type of gift or favor with an arrogant, disrespectful attitude? Probably not, and you shouldn't ask for forgiveness with such an attitude either. And importantly, you need to do your part. Do the following before seeking your partner's forgiveness.

- Forgive those who have hurt you. Jesus addressed this situation with the parable of the unforgiving debtor in Matthew 18:23–35, where a debtor whose debts had been forgiven refused to forgive another's debt. When the king heard about what had happened, he called his debtor before him and said, "You evil-hearted wretch! Here I forgave you all that tremendous debt, just because you asked me to—shouldn't you have mercy on others, just as I had mercy on you?" However, forgiving one who has hurt you doesn't mean you have earned or deserve their forgiveness in return. It only sets the stage for you to ask for it.

- Prepare for forgiveness by being clear about the offense(s) that is of concern: understand specifically what you have done that is making you feel guilt and shame that requires forgiveness. Know that you are truly remorseful—you feel an honest, deep, and painful regret for what you did. A good way to do this is to tell your story—what you have done and how you feel—to yourself, to a trusted friend, or to your journal.

- Accept responsibility for what you have done. You cannot accept another person's forgiveness if you deny that you are a cause of a problem or that your behavior has offended someone. Ask yourself why there is a problem, and what its direct effect and ripple effects have been.

- Consider who you are accountable to as a way of deciding from whom you need to seek forgiveness. If you have hurt or offended someone you are accountable to, then their forgiveness is important. You will probably conclude that you are accountable to God, to yourself, to the person you abused, and to others. That's who you probably need to seek forgiveness from.

- Confess to God, yourself, and to others. Admit you have been wrong and acknowledge or disclose your misdeeds, faults, or sins. You will need to confess these actions to God, yourself, and to the person you want to forgive you. Review Chapter 9 and 10 for more about confession.

- Repent. What story have you been living—the one where you see yourself as a victim, concerned only with "me," behaving badly, dominating and abusing others? If so, what should your life look like instead? Are you committed to real change—a U-turn—in your life? Can you now live a story of positive intention, optimism, and hope rather than bad behavior, without abusing anyone? Review Chapter 4 for more about repentance and transforming your life.

- Look ahead to restitution. Restitution involves giving back, or making right the wrong you have done. Making restitution will go a long way toward helping with forgiveness. Restitution is discussed in Chapter 13.

When There Is No Forgiveness

Remember that forgiving you may be very difficult or impossible for the person you have hurt, particularly a partner you have abused. Trust may have been broken so badly that nothing will make the situation better. Even asking her to forgive you might be considered an arrogant insult. Theologian L. Gregory Jones has written;

> . . . the patterns of diminution and destruction that are deeply embedded in our lives and in our structures, make the craft of forgiveness difficult if not—at least in some circumstances, in some lives—either impossible or morally unjustified. This is even more the case when those who are powerful use forgiveness as a weapon to keep their subjects powerless or when the lack of repentance by the offender(s) suggests that the offense(s) will persist or perhaps even become exacerbated.[9]

Thus before asking for forgiveness, empathize with the person whose forgiveness you are seeking. Walk in her shoes and don't insult her. Remember that sometimes the hurt has been so bad, things have gone so far, that "I'm sorry," or "Please forgive me," no matter how often repeated, will not make any difference. They almost seem to make everything worse. The person you have abused may not have the ability to let go of her pain, anger, disappointment, and suffering. She may not forgive you.

The reason doesn't matter. When you, as an abuser, are not granted forgiveness for your mistakes, you have to accept this. If you've been honest, asked humbly for forgiveness, and done whatever you can to make the situation better, you've done all you can do. If your abused partner cannot or will not accept your request, you can go no further.

The pain of not being forgiven cuts deep, sometimes much deeper than the guilt and pain that are driving the hope for forgiveness. But when the wreckage from your past stares you in the face and forgiveness is not to be granted, there's nothing more you can do. Going back and rewriting the past is impossible. Your responsibility then is to yourself and those with whom you do have a relationship. You need to put one foot in front of the other and hold your head high with the knowledge you will not abuse again, and that you will be the best person that you can be. All you can do is to move forward, learn from it, and let go.

Questions for Reflection or Group Study

1. If you do not forgive a person who has hurt you, what happens to you?

2. List three people who have hurt you or you have a grudge against and briefly explain the situation.

3. What should you do with respect to each of those persons?

4. Think of an example of abuse. Who was abused? For what actions might the person who abused seek forgiveness?

5. Do you want any person to forgive you? If so, who and why?

6. What do you need to do before you ask a person to forgive you?

7. What should you do if a person from whom you want forgiveness does not forgive you?

> ### Personal Reflection
>
> Which of the learning objectives for this chapter is most important to you in stopping abuse and transforming your life? Why?

CHAPTER 13
Restitution

Learning Objectives

After completing this chapter, you should be able to:
- Explain the difference between court imposed and voluntary restitution.
- Make restitution to God.
- Explain how you can become a whole person.
- Make amends to the victim of your abuse for the physical and material damage you did to her.
- Make symbolic restitution for the psychological, mental, and spiritual damage you did to your victim.

JOEL AND CHRISTY ARE BOTH TWENTY-NINE years old, have been together for ten years, married for five. Their first years were generally peaceful, though occasionally Joel tried to tell Christy how to live her life, and from time to time they engaged in pretty bad verbal fights. After the birth of their first child, the relationship seemed to go downhill. Joel became verbally and emotionally abusive, and Christy's life became a nightmare. Some time ago Joel began to get physical. He pushed Christy into a wall and slammed a door in her face when he got upset after she asked him to help with the baby. On another occasion he berated Christy for "nagging," and after about an hour of verbal abuse smashed a glass at her feet and grabbed her in a chokehold, frightening her badly. Later, when Christy asked for help with the baby, Joel jumped on top of her and forced his knees into her back, then followed her around the house for about thirty minutes verbally abusing and occasionally slapping her—and badly bruising her face.

Christy finally left their home and moved in with her parents in their small, overcrowded house. Joel is living in their apartment and continuing in his job. Sometimes he sees Christy and their baby on weekends.

Christy is having a difficult time. Living with her parents creates problems, but she can't afford her own apartment. She needs to see a doctor for her continuing headaches, but doesn't because she can't pay the bill. She can't find a job that would allow her to pay for child care and make ends meet. She is not sleeping well and is becoming more and more isolated from her friends.

Joel is in a twenty-four-week program for domestic batterers and has attended a local church several times on Sunday morning. He feels badly about the way he treated Christy. He cannot explain his behavior, even to himself. Joel wants to make things right. After learning about restitution, Joel has decided he needs to make amends to Christy, but he's not sure what to do or how to do it. He is so mixed up.

About Restitution

Jesus told a story of restitution in Luke 19. The Romans had levied heavy taxes against all under their control. The Jews opposed these taxes but were still forced to pay. The tax collectors, who often made themselves rich by swindling their fellow Jews, were among the most unpopular people in Israel. Zacchaeus was one of the hated tax collectors. In spite of this, Jesus went home with him and loved him. Zacchaeus stood before the Lord and said, "Look, Lord! Here and now I give half of my possessions to the poor, and if I have cheated anybody out of anything, I will pay back four times the amount." By giving to the poor and paying back to those he had cheated, Zacchaeus made restitution and showed internal change by outward action.

In its traditional sense, restitution has been defined as a monetary payment by an offender to the victim for the harm resulting from an offense. In this sense, restitution in a domestic violence case involves compensation for physical and material losses suffered by a victim that a court orders an abuser to pay as a condition of probation. It might cover economic damages suffered by the victim, such as medical bills, lost income, counseling or therapy costs, or other economic costs incurred because of the abuse. Court ordered restitution may be appropriate in some cases. In any case, however, it only addresses part of the total "cost" of the abuse.

Abuse always leaves deep scars that go well beyond the physical and material damage that a court can address. The scars include psychological effects such as damage to the victim's self-esteem; physical consequences such as sleeping problems, digestive issues, headaches, hypertension; and social consequences, where victims isolate themselves, stop seeing friends and family, and feel unworthy and ashamed. Addressing such issues can be overwhelming, and require a long and difficult healing process in the victim's search for peace.

Restitution for this type of hurt and pain goes beyond what courts can require. It is what you need to voluntarily do to make amends for all the harm you have done, and to support your victim in her physical, emotional, spiritual, social, and financial healing process. It involves justice and fair treatment, not personal gain for you or a way of trying to control the other person. It is the right thing to do.

In making amends through restitution, you are acknowledging and admitting that you were at fault and that you caused harm to the victim. Restitution aims to help the victim repair her life, and also should foster a spiritual awakening that helps you transform your life. To truly make amends for abuse, you need to make restitution to God, yourself, and to your victim(s).

Make Restitution to God

As Joel reflected on his situation, he concluded that his relationship with God was similar to his relationship with Christy. He was a believer and at one time felt he had a pretty good relationship with God. But he had not had an active faith in several years, and was now more estranged from God than from Christy. Joel believed he needed to repair his relationship with God. To do this, he needed to make amends to God.

What does it mean to hurt God? Leviticus 6:2–5 tells us we hurt God when we hurt or offend our fellow man:

> If anyone sins and is unfaithful to the Lord by deceiving a neighbor about something entrusted to them or left in their care or about something stolen, or if they cheat their neighbor, or if they find lost property and lie about it, or if they swear falsely about any such sin that people may commit—when they sin in any of these ways and realize their guilt, they must return what they have stolen or taken by extortion, or what was entrusted to them, or the lost property they found, or whatever it was they swore falsely about. They must make restitution in full, add a fifth of the value to it and give it all to the owner on the day they present their guilt offering.

How do we make restitution to God when we have hurt Him? We make restitution to God when we care for and make restitution to those people we have hurt or offended. Matthew 25:37–40 tells us how love for others is love for God:

Then the righteous will answer him, 'Lord, when did we see you hungry and feed you, or thirsty and give you something to drink? When did we see you a stranger and invite you in, or needing clothes and clothe you? When did we see you sick or in prison and go to visit you?' The King will reply, 'Truly I tell you, whatever you did for one of the least of these brothers and sisters of mine, you did for me.'

Thus we make amends to God when we care for others: for the small people of the world, the needy, the poor, those who cannot return our care and concern, and those we have offended and hurt. Certainly making amends to a partner we have abused is a way of making restitution to God. Joel can make restitution to God by making amends to Christy or others he has hurt.

Make Restitution to Self

Making restitution to self at first seems like an opportunity to reward yourself—to go on a shopping spree, or take the afternoon off work, or just have a favorite ice cream. Restitution is not a reward however, and such superficial actions don't heal our hurt or brokenness.

So how do you make restitution to yourself? One way is to do what you can to become a whole person. People describe a whole person differently, and you need to think about your own definition. I Thessalonians 5:23 speaks of a whole person as being whole in spirit, soul, and body. A view that fits well for this discussion is of a person who is fully connected to their own and others' humanity, and has a proper balance in all aspects of his life—for example, he spends meaningful time with family and friends, fosters good and healthy relationships, maintains his health, becomes all he can be, gives back to his community, manages his financial affairs, and grows in his spiritual life. If your life is missing such things, it is not in balance, and you are probably not completely whole.

Making restitution to yourself and becoming more whole means addressing one or more of the missing elements in your life, and moving one step at a time toward your own wholeness. It can include elements that are opposites of brokenness, such as:

- You behave as humans are expected to behave.
- You have positive relationships with your partner, relatives, and friends.
- You have a rich spiritual life.
- You love.
- You have hope.
- You see and understand beauty.
- You are thankful.
- You feel empathy and compassion.
- You choose not to hurt others.
- You forgive and don't hold grudges.

Add your own elements that are necessary for a whole life for you. What does your complete list look like?

Make Restitution to Abuse Victims

When you abuse another person, you take or withhold something that is rightfully theirs. When Joel abused Christy, he took away many things. Some are clear, like her home, her financial stability, and probably her health. Other things he took from her are just as real, but are harder to describe and measure, like her freedom, her sense of well-being, and her confidence in her own humanity.

To make restitution, Joel needs to make every effort to help Christy become, to the extent possible, like she was before he abused her: financially, mentally, physically, and emotionally. He needs to repay those things to her that he can, and try to create an environment that will help her deal with other parts of her healing process. To accomplish this will probably require him to make two forms of restitution.

Pay Direct Restitution

As noted above, abuse directly takes from victims many specific, measurable physical or material things, like their health and their financial stability. Your abuse may have caused your partner to incur doctor or counselor bills, lose her job, have additional child care costs, and such. Restitution includes returning or compensating for such things: for example, making her whole financially, handling her medical bills, voluntarily paying child support, or meeting other of her needs. The idea is that you should do all you can to minimize your partner's physical and material suffering from the consequences of your abusive actions. You should be willing to repay her for the consequences to the extent that doing so is possible.

Make Symbolic Restitution

Abuse also has equally bad consequences that are less identifiable and measurable, harder to discern, and generally not conducive to direct restitution: mental and psychological effects such as post-traumatic stress disorder, depression, prolonged sadness, fear of intimacy, anxiety, and low self-esteem; substance abuse; and emotional and spiritual issues such as hopelessness, emotional detachment, feeling worthless, feeling discouraged about the future, or questioning one's spiritual faith.

As an abuser who caused such pain, you cannot directly pay the victim back for such damage or fix the problems you have caused. But you can always offer restitution, even for your verbal, psychological, emotional, physical, or sexual abuse of your partner. You can engage in a form of what has been called "symbolic restitution." Where direct payback is not possible, you can do things that don't directly relate to the consequences of the abuse, but that provide social value and are indirectly related to the consequences. Such symbolic restitution says to the victim, "I'm taking responsibility, and you are not to blame. I'm doing this for you, even though not directly."

The main thing you can do to offer symbolic restitution is to accept responsibility for your actions and fix yourself. You can stop abusing and transform your life. You can demonstrate the elements of wholeness listed above, as well as others that are important to you. Such a change on your part will communicate to your victim that she has been heard, believed, and validated. It will foster an environment where she can move toward healing.

The details of restitution will vary from case to case, and each individual situation will require something different. In the case of Joel and Christy, Joel needs to offer direct restitution for Christy's additional economic burdens. And he needs to provide symbolic restitution for her psychological and emotional burdens by stopping all abuse and transforming his life to one of wholeness. In doing this, he may engage in elements of community service or community restitution designed to expand his understanding of family violence and to have him involved in its prevention.

Subjects covered in other chapters of this book logically and naturally lead to symbolic restitution: accepting responsibility, acknowledging accountability, confessing, and forgiving and seeking forgiveness are all steps that tell you why you need to make restitution and to whom, and help establish an environment in which making amends is feasible. Other chapters address how you need to behave going forward to live as a whole person and make symbolic restitution to your victim. It is up to you to look at yourself, your partner, and your situation, and decide what to do.

RESTITUTION

Questions for Reflection or Group Study

1. When you abuse someone how do you hurt God?

2. What should you do to make amends to God?

3. Describe yourself if you are a "whole" person. What elements do you add to the list discussed in the narrative above?

4. List four specific things you can do to become a more whole person?

5. Complete the following chart by listing five examples of incidents when your actions hurt your partner or failed to meet her physical or material needs, and then state what you should do to make amends.

Hurt or Failed to Meet Her Needs	Make Amends
1.	1.
2.	2.
3.	3.
4.	4.
5.	5.

RESTITUTION

6. How can symbolic restitution help—

   an abuse victim?

   you?

> ## Personal Reflection
>
> Which of the learning objectives for this chapter is most important to you in stopping abuse and transforming your life? Why?

CHAPTER 14
Reconciliation

Learning Objectives

After completing this chapter, you should be able to:
- See that you can reconcile with God by being His friend.
- Reconcile with yourself by acknowledge conflict within your own being and making peace among the conflicting parts of you.
- Consider the type of relationship that is most appropriate for reconciling with your partner.
- Establish an environment where reconciliation with an abused partner might be possible.

JOEL (INTRODUCED IN CHAPTER 13) LOOKED deeply at himself and acknowledged his abuse. He is taking steps to make restitution to God, himself, and Christy. Christy and he are still living apart, but he loves her and would like to re-establish a marital relationship and provide a peaceful family environment for their child. He knows it will be tough. Christy is on the fence about getting back together, and her family, who view Joel as a monster, are strongly opposed. They counsel her to never return to him because it is never going to be safe. They tell her things like, "Once an abuser always an abuser," "If he hits you once he'll hit you twice," and "Abusers don't change." Even so, Joel would like to find peace with Christy, her family, and others he has hurt.

Joel is not sure whether Christy wants to repair their relationship. Even if she wants things to return to where they were, she will be torn by loyalty to her family and by fear for her personal safety if she agrees to try to get together. Joel has begun to make amends for what he has done—by attending church regularly and voluntarily paying her medical costs and some child support. He is not sure where their relationship will go.

About Reconciliation

We most often think of reconciliation as the coming together of two people, perhaps two who have been estranged. It can mean restoring an estranged relationship. It can also cover a range of situations such as settling a quarrel or difference, reaching an agreement, changing conflict into peaceful coexistence, becoming friends or sometimes re-establishing a loving, intimate relationship. As with restitution, you will need to reconcile with God, self, and others,

Reconcile with God

Reconciling with God is necessary for Joel to repair his relationship with Him. James 2:23 describes how God reconciles himself to us and how we can be reconciled with Him by being His friend: "And the Scripture was fulfilled that says, 'Abraham believed God, and it was credited to him as righteousness,' and he was called God's friend."

What does it mean to be a friend of God? That's a question about which volumes could be written. Let's think, however, of a few simple characteristics of our own friendship with other people and see what it tells us about how we can reconcile with God.

- Friends have affection for one another and try to live in harmony. We are not perfect, and never will be, but we all have the ability to love God and try to live in harmony with Him. If we do, we are becoming His friend.

- Friends are not here today and gone tomorrow. Nothing stands in the way of their relationship, and they stick it out through thick and thin, are not alienated or estranged, and don't hold grudges. The same is true for God if you are His friend.

- Friends communicate with one another. Communicating with God means reading and studying His word and talking to Him in prayer. You ask for His help and thank Him for it. You acknowledge your true condition, recognize His power, and give Him room to work in your life.

- Friends try to please one another. If we are God's friend, we aim to please Him and do what He wants us to do rather than what we would like to do. We surrender to His will and please him by living for His purpose, abiding by His commandments, and giving Him the glory.

These four simple principles of friendship—showing affection, maintaining the relationship through all the ups and downs, communicating, and pleasing God by surrendering to his will—can go a long way toward your reconciling with God and pave the way for your reconciliation with human beings.

Reconcile with Self

What does it mean to have a bad relationship with yourself: a relationship that needs repair? We take it to mean that your humanity is broken, and the parts are in a war with one another. Think of Joel. His abusive behavior, his choice to hurt his wife and others, suggests he does not have a loving spirit or a will to behave as a discerning human being. He is also hurting—when he really thinks about himself, he is filled with shame and remorse. At his core he is a decent human being, capable of nonviolence, peace, and love. But his desire for control and his choices to dominate and abuse have led him to hurt those he loves, and in doing so to be seen as a monster. He wants to be a decent human being, but he continues to choose to abuse Christy. Joel is broken, and the two sides of his humanity are at war with one another.

To repair the relationship between the two parts of himself, Joel needs to reconcile with himself. Reconciling with self can mean various things, but above all it means being at peace with yourself. To gain peace with yourself, you need to recognize and acknowledge conflict within your own being—that you have many good attributes but also confusion about who you really are, and perhaps some negative attributes such as failure to acknowledge responsibility for your behavior, letting desire to be in control take charge of your life, resentment or hatred toward others, guilt or shame for what you've done, emptiness or other destructive feelings and emotions. To resolve this internal conflict and reconcile with yourself, you need to recognize that both sides of you exist and be honest about your whole life.

There is no magic formula for resolving your internal conflict and reconciling with yourself. Doing so is often a long and difficult journey where you need help from a friend, spiritual advisor, or professional counselor. In simple terms however, reconciling with yourself boils down to making peace within yourself by changing the part of you that you don't much like. Fostering peace, internally and with others, is a principal purpose of this book. Let's briefly review several of its teachings as a road map for a process of personal reconciliation.

- Remember that God loves you, will help you, and through Him there is hope. Pray to Him and seek His help in your reconciliation effort.

- Clarify who you are, emphasizing the parts you like and the parts you don't like. Take responsibility for your behavior and its consequences and be accountable to your own conscience.

- Be honest with yourself about the part of you that you like, the part that you don't like, and who you are. Confess to yourself about the part you don't like.

- Forgive yourself by accepting God's forgiveness.

- Repent, or commit to change the parts you don't like and transform your life. Think about the type of relationship you want with God and with your fellow human beings. Think about what peace means to you and the type of person you need to be to bring peace into your life.

- Establish goals for your life and then change the parts of you that don't foster those goals.

Making peace with yourself is not an easy assignment, but you can do it with God's help. When you do, you have reconciled with yourself. You are then ready to move on.

Reconcile with Others

Reconciliation is a choice, not an inevitability. It is only appropriate if both parties want it to happen. Further, it doesn't happen all at once and may take a long time. Tearing down a brick wall by hand is a good metaphor for reconciling. Think of you and your partner as being separated by a brick wall. You cannot get over it, go around it, or blast your way through it. The only thing you can do is to slowly, gradually break the mortar, remove one brick at a time, and keep removing one brick at a time until the wall is low enough that you can get to the other side.

Reconciling after abuse is a similar process, but it needs to start with you stopping the abuse. Then hopefully, you can work one step at a time to tear down the wall of pain and suffering that resulted when you chose to abuse her.

Tearing down the wall will almost surely include fixing the unequal power structure that no doubt existed in your relationship. Your power—the power that probably caused the breakup—will also affect your efforts at reconciliation. You may try to hold on to the power. And the disparity of power will probably prohibit the use of couple's therapy to address the issue. There is a great risk for any person who is being abused to attend therapy with their abusive partner, as the person who abused may use what is said in therapy later against them.

Reconciling with an abused partner is not always possible. You and the victim of your abuse have to agree whether reconciliation is possible, and if so, what form it should take. In the case of domestic abuse, reconciliation does not necessarily mean having a romantic relationship or living together. Instead, it may have either of several results, which often change and evolve over time. Following are some possible examples:

- Stop the abuse and coexist in peace.
- Live separately and don't fight.
- Peacefully co-parent kids.
- Sincerely agree to work toward an improved relationship.
- Get a peaceful divorce.
- Maintain a loving, intimate relationship.
- Others as appropriate.

In summary, reconciling with a victim of your abuse involves developing a relationship of nonviolence and peace where she feels safe, and that each of you agrees is in her best interest and appropriate for both of you. It can take any of various forms, and may change from one to another over time. Below are some thoughts on creating an environment that fosters reconciliation, deciding when to try, and discerning how to go about it and what you hope the result will be.

Establish the Environment

Fostering an environment for reconciliation is your starting point. You are the only person you can control, and trying to force your desires on another person (the essence of domestic abuse in the first place) most often leads, not to reconciliation, but to even further conflict, estrangement, and anger. This is particularly true in the case of domestic abuse, where essentially all trust is gone and your partner is likely to be fearful for both her emotional and physical safety. All you can do is control your own behavior and behave in ways that your partner might want to reconcile with you. The following will go a long way toward creating such an environment.

- Pray for your partner and for the success of your endeavor. Prayer brings her into your heart, helps you empathize, breaks down the hostility and distinction between her and you, and begins to make her into a friend. Praying for God's help in your reconciliation will also help give you the courage to attempt what can be a difficult and risky endeavor.

- Build trust. Lack of trust is probably the biggest impediment to reconciliation, and to have true reconciliation, you have to develop mutual trust, as discussed in Chapter 23. Trust requires honesty, and never promising to change and then failing to do so.

- Demonstrate humility rather than false pride or arrogance. Humility requires seeing yourself as you are, warts and all. To reconcile, you need to be humble, not just in the sense of being gentle or meek, but also being vulnerable and willing to be hurt. You have to be willing to go unnoticed, to be the last, to receive the least.

Decide When to Invite Reconciliation

After you have done your best to create an environment for reconciliation, you still face the question of whether or when to actually attempt to reconcile. Deciding when to seek reconciliation and what you hope to accomplish is a personal decision for you and your partner, and it must be a mutual decision where both parties agree, without any pressure, manipulation, or coercion at all. For your part, ask yourself questions such as:

- How have I harmed my partner, and how is this a barrier to reconciliation? How does my abuse prevent her from wanting to reconcile?

- Can my partner and I each reflect carefully, objectively, and honestly on our relationship and look at the big picture?

- Have I accepted responsibility for choosing to abuse my partner, remembering that nothing she did could have justified the abuse?

- In what ways am I accountable to her? Do I acknowledge that accountability?

- Have I repented and committed to change? If not, is any form of reconciliation feasible or appropriate?

- Am I prepared to deliver on my commitment to change, without reservation?

- Have I reconciled with myself?

- Have I reconciled with God?

- Does my partner want to reconcile? Are the effects of the abuse still so raw that reconciliation is difficult or impossible?

- When I listen, empathize, and care deeply about my partner's situation can I discern that she is able to reconcile?

Positive answers to such questions suggest that an agreement to coexist in nonviolence, peace, and mutuality with a partner is feasible. Without the correct answers, any attempt to reconcile may initially appear to work but will probably lead to frustration, manipulation, coercion, and violence.

Seek Reconciliation When Appropriate

Seeking reconciliation requires you to examine your past use of violence, commit not to repeat it, and start from where you are. The following guidelines will apply in most situations:

- Consider talking about talking. Make an overture and determine whether reconciliation is even something she would like to discuss. If the door is open, you may find it helpful to send a letter or email proposing that you and your partner agree to have preparatory discussions before you actually start to discuss your differences.

- Go slow. Paradoxically, you often need to go slow in order to move toward reconciliation, and you may need to move from one form to another over time. Both of you may need time to think about what is happening, adjust to changes, overlook some small issues, accept some disappointments. Taking your time, taking one small step at a time, may be necessary in a reconciliation journey in such situations.

- Try to engage in dialogue and tell and listen to your stories. Don't rehash the past as a way of casting blame, but discuss it as a way of understanding her humanity and preparing a path for the future.

- Listen with empathy. To reconcile, you need to understand your partner's needs, feelings, and emotions, and walk in her shoes. Listening with empathy will allow this to happen.

- Validate your partner. Acknowledge her humanity and value as a fellow human being. Regardless of the conflict, you can always find something positive to say. Say it.

- Address your own responsibility and accountability. Confess and repent with a sincere apology. Honestly acknowledging your own mistakes is a sign of your strength and maturity, and doing so will set the stage for a candid discussion. And mean it. Nothing is worse than claiming to change and then reverting to your former behavior.

- Seek a win/win resolution, as discussed in Chapter 24. Most reconciliations involve differences where both people have interests that need to be addressed. Repairing the relationship is not likely, and reconciliation is not likely to last or be productive, if one person wins and the other loses. Instead, both people need to feel a sense of fairness, even if the issues between you are not always resolved. Reconciliation is about restoring relationships, not getting your way.

- Accept your partner as she is. Remember that you are trying to stop abusing her and transform your life, not fix your partner.

Reconciliation to a close or intimate relationship isn't always possible or appropriate, regardless of how much you work for it, hope for it, or pray for it. Reconciling takes two people, and sometimes two people just cannot get together in a close relationship. But all broken relationships can, with good faith, be repaired so that each person can live as a whole, functioning human being, in peace with the other. Appropriate reconciliation provides a journey for such peace.

RECONCILIATION

Questions for Reflection or Group Study

1. Describe your relationship with God.

2. List four specific things you can do to become a better friend with God.

3. Describe the two sides of your humanity by listing three good things about yourself and three things you don't much like about yourself.

Good Things About Myself	Things I Don't Like About Myself
1.	1.
2.	2.
3.	3.

4. Do you intend to reconcile with your partner? Explain.

5. What type of reconciliation is most feasible in your case?

6. List at least five things you should do to create an environment that fosters reconciliation.

7. How might the relationship change if you and your partner reconcile?

Personal Reflection

Which of the learning objectives for this chapter is most important to you in stopping abuse and transforming your life? Why?

PART THREE
Maintaining Peace

MAKE GOOD CHOICES

CHAPTER 15

Anger

Learning Objectives

After completing this chapter, you should be able to:
- Distinguish between helpful anger and that which is negative and destructive.
- Appreciate that abuse is caused by desire to maintain power and control, not by anger.
- Determine whether your anger is a problem in your relationships.
- Identify your beliefs that are leading to anger and begin to change them.
- Take actions to manage your anger and prevent it from escalating.

ANGER SURFACES IN MOST DOMESTIC ABUSE situations. Let's look at the case of Kenneth and Laura. Laura's ten-year-old daughter by a previous marriage suddenly became very ill with an extremely high fever. Laura missed work and spent the day at her bedside, then took her to see a doctor. Failing an immediate diagnosis, her daughter was admitted to a hospital. Laura spent every waking hour at her bedside, returning home only to bathe and change clothes, and occasionally for a short, fitful sleep. What little conversation she had with Kenneth was about her daughter and her concern for her. She spent a great deal of time on the phone, discussing the matter with a friend who happened to be a nurse. Kenneth handled most of the first day okay, but after that his blood began to boil. On the second day he exploded, yelling at Laura, "Why the hell are you gone all the time? There's nothing you can do but sit up there and flirt with the doctors. And even when you are here, it's like I don't exist." Then he charged out, slamming the door into Laura and "accidently" bruising the side of her face.

About Anger

Anger is a strong feeling of displeasure and usually of antagonism that frequently occurs when things don't go your way, you don't get what you want, or you feel hurt.

Anger is not inherently negative. Some anger is a normal emotional reaction that may energize us, motivate us to solve problems that are negatively affecting us, or drive us toward positive change, but not everyone uses violence against their intimate partner. Ephesians 4:26 states, "In your anger do not sin: Do not let the sun go down while you are still angry," and James 1:19 reads, "My dear brothers and sisters, take note of this: Everyone should be quick to listen, slow to speak and slow to become angry."

However, anger is a negative force when it is caused by unacceptable beliefs and expectations—such as an inappropriate belief that you have a right to control your partner. Anger is also negative when you use it to justify your abuse, hurt yourself or others, or damage property. Longer-term, unresolved anger leads to resentment and bitterness. It can damage your relationships, health, career, and overall enjoyment of life. You need to understand your anger and then deal with it.

Understand Your Anger

A myth holds that anger causes abuse. While most abuse involves an element of anger, anger is a consequence—an effect—of an abusive attitude rather than a cause of abuse. Your anger does not cause you to abuse others. Anger is one of your tools for controlling others and getting what you want.

How do you know whether you are abusive or angry? Consider the following:

- Is anger a problem for you outside the home? If not, this suggests you know how to express anger civilly, if you choose to do so, and angry behavior at home is a form of abuse.

- Do you ever use cruel, intimidating, manipulative, controlling or physically violent actions toward your partner when you are not angry? If so, desire for control, not anger, is the reason for your abuse.

- Do you ever use other tactics, such as expressions of jealousy, frustration, fear of abandonment, or even love, to control your partner or children? If so, abuse, not anger, is your problem.

- Do you ever use your anger as a weapon—on purpose to remind your partner and children that it is dangerous to cross you? If so, you may be using anger as a tool of abuse.

If you are involved in partner abuse, you are unlikely to take responsibility for your anger or your actions. Let's look at the question of responsibility.

Look at Cause and Effect

People frequently think anger causes abuse because they think that if two things happen about the same time or in a predictable order, the first causes the second. This type of thinking might suggest that because Kenneth got angry, he abused Laura.

Think more deeply about Kenneth and Laura. Kenneth got angry. He abused Laura. But did Kenneth abuse Laura because he was angry? The fact is that anger did not cause Kenneth's abuse and does not cause domestic abuse. A man's attitude, abusive beliefs, and expectations are responsible for his abuse.

This situation is illustrated on the right. In this case, Kenneth didn't abuse Laura because he was angry. He was abusive because he had unrealistic, inappropriate expectations of her and they were not being met. He felt entitled to dominate Laura and to demand she devote her time to him, regardless of the circumstances. When Laura didn't meet his demands and submit to his control, Kenneth let his anger take over. He was not abusive because he was angry. He used anger to justify his abuse when his wife didn't put him first during this crisis.

Do A "Why" Analysis

Let's look at Kenneth's anger by asking a series of "why" questions, as discussed in more detail in Chapter 5. Asking why questions helps discover the underlying, root, causes of a situation: the basic reason(s) for the occurrence.

Domestic Abuse and Anger

Abuser believes he has the right to control and dominate his partner

Abuser uses controlling, abusive actions

Abusive actions fail: Abuser doesn't get what he wants

Abuser becomes angry

Abuser escalates the abuse and fails to take responsibility

Using why questions to determine who or what caused Kenneth's abusive behavior involves identifying the abusive event and then looking back in time and asking and honestly answering a series of questions:

- What did Kenneth do? He yelled at Laura and slammed the door into her.

- Why did Kenneth yell at Laura and slam the door into her? Because he was angry.

- Why was Kenneth angry? Because he felt Laura was ignoring him.

- Why did Kenneth believe Laura was unfairly ignoring him? Because he believed he was entitled to control Laura and her behavior.

Asking why will usually show that when you are angry and abuse your partner, you do so because your beliefs convinced you that you were entitled to control her, she didn't go along, and you used your anger to control her and try to get your way. This approach has probably worked in the past, so you expect that there will be no adverse consequences for you.

Deal With Your Anger

Fixing your "anger problems" requires more than a quick fix, such as a short-term change of behavior, feeling sorry for your actions, an insincere apology, a promise that abuse will never happen again, or attending an anger management program. Instead, you need to make a deeper, more real change, and in doing so address the underlying, root cause of your anger, which typically is your abusive belief system. Really dealing with your anger requires you to change your beliefs, which should lead to a change in your behavior.

Minimize Anger by Changing Your Beliefs

As discussed in more detail in Chapter 1, the core, central belief that causes abusive behavior is the belief that it's okay for you to control another person. This core belief is usually expressed in a several related beliefs, such as:

- Entitlement, or your belief that you have a special status and rights.

- Selfishness and or self-centeredness, or your lack of consideration for others, and being concerned chiefly with your desires.

- Superiority, your exaggerated feeling of being superior to or better than your partner.

- Disrespect, which follows from a feeling of superiority.

- Possessiveness, when you want to own, possess, dominate, or control your partner, and view her as a material object instead of a human being.

- Confusing love and abuse, when you try to justify control as an expression of your deep love.

If you hold beliefs such as these or other similar ones, you are likely to become angry if your partner does not do what you want her to do. Truly dealing with your anger requires you to look at your beliefs from your partner's point of view—to empathize with her—and change them to ones that consider her and others' best interests, such as:

- You and your partner have equal status and rights.

- You consider your partner's needs and desires as equal to yours.

- You believe you are not better than or above your partner.

- You respect your partner.

- You do not own your partner, and you treat her as a human being rather than an object.

- You show love because you love her.

Seeing the world through your partner's eyes, empathizing with her, and changing your thinking patterns along these lines should reduce the likelihood you will use anger to justify your abuse. Your expectations will be fulfilled, removing anything to be angry about.

Manage Your Anger

Changing your beliefs should help you address your anger. However, sometimes you may want to believe differently, but deep-seated abusive beliefs surface and you become angry in spite of your efforts to the contrary. And sometimes, as noted above, there are other reasons, perhaps legitimate, for feeling angry.

Regardless of the reason, if you are angry you need to change your behavior from that which controls and abuses to behavior that fosters nonviolence, peace, and equality. Skills such as the following will help you reduce the likelihood of using anger as a justification to hurt, control, or further abuse your partner.

- Identify situations that are likely to set you off, and respond in nonaggressive ways.

- Slow down your arousal when you are angry, so that it can be processed and acted on in a proper, constructive, and healthy way.

- Develop specific thinking patterns and skills for dealing with situations likely to trigger anger.

- Calm down when beginning to feel upset.

- Express feelings and needs without being aggressive.

- Focus on problem-solving instead of using energy to be angry.

- Communicate effectively to diffuse anger and resolve conflicts.

These types of skills can be complex and you may need professional help in dealing with them. Anger management classes may be appropriate under certain circumstances. However, if you are using abusive behavior, such programs need to challenge your underlying beliefs that cause you to use anger to control your partner, and teach you to take responsibility for how you hurt others with your anger. Accordingly, focusing only on anger management is not likely to help you over the long term, as this typically does not address the root cause of abuse, which is your unrelenting effort to control the thoughts, feelings and actions of another human being. While "anger management" may be an appropriate addition to your efforts, you mainly need to address the beliefs that lead to your abuse.

ANGER

Questions for Reflection or Group Study

1. Describe a situation in which you were angry with your partner and used that anger to justify abusing her. Include some detail, such as what happened, the partner's response, the consequences, etc.

   a. Describe the situation.

   b. Why did you act as you did in this example? What were you thinking?

   c. If you were angry, why were you angry?

d. What belief(s) do you think led to the anger?

e. What other choices did you have for dealing with the situation?

2. List four beliefs abusive men often hold about women that may be the root cause of their anger.

ANGER

3. Chapter 5 discussed four "unhealthy approaches" to responsibility, listed below. State how you may use them to try to avoid responsibility for your anger.

   Minimizing

   Denying

   Rationalizing

   Blaming

4. List several pros and cons of you participating in an anger management program.

   Pros:

   Cons:

5. What do you need to do to manage your anger?

Personal Reflection

Which of the learning objectives for this chapter is most important to you in stopping abuse and transforming your life? Why?

CHAPTER 16

Substance Abuse

Learning Objectives

After completing this chapter, you should be able to:
- Recognize that any excessive, inappropriate, illegal, or harmful use of a mind-altering substance, such as alcohol, drugs, or certain household items, is substance abuse.
- Understand that use and abuse of alcohol and drugs do not cause domestic abuse, but instead contribute to escalating abusive incidents or make abuse worse.
- Distinguish between domestic abuse and substance abuse.
- Assess your behavior, and determine whether you have a substance abuse problem.
- Pursue plans and appropriate programs to deal with each type of abuse.

A *HOUSTON CHRONICLE* ARTICLE ENTITLED, "Mississippi leaders: Official must go if he hit wife," explained, "Second-term [legislator] was arrested during the weekend and charged with misdemeanor domestic violence. Sheriff's deputies said [the legislator] bloodied his wife's nose after she didn't undress quickly enough when [the legislator] wanted to have sex, . . . Deputies reported [the legislator] was drunk when they arrived at the couple's home late Saturday."[10]

Did the legislator have a drinking problem, or an abuse problem, or both?

About Substance Abuse

The man mentioned in the *Chronicle* was drunk, indicating he had a problem with substance abuse. Substance abuse generally is defined as a pattern of excessive, inappropriate, illegal, or harmful use of a substance such as alcohol or drugs (whether legal or illegal). Substance abuse results from using a substance in a way that is not intended or recommended, or using it more than prescribed. You are abusing substances, whether or not you are addicted, if your use causes significant impairment in your daily life, such as health or disability issues, failure to meet responsibilities, or breakdown of social relationships. If your use causes you to have hangovers, miss work or school, lose friends; or if you take more than you intend to, your use is probably at the abuse level.

Substance and Domestic Abuse

Chapter 15 noted that "A myth holds that anger causes abuse," when in fact abusive attitudes cause anger. Similarly, people often believe that alcohol and substance abuse cause domestic abuse, as one might conclude in the case above where the legislator was drunk when he hit his wife. However this is another myth. The fact that things happen about the same time or in the same order does not mean that the first causes the second. And substance abuse does not cause domestic abuse just because an abuser is drunk.

Men who abuse others are violent and controlling, whether they are intoxicated or not, as domestic abuse is a learned behavior, resulting from the man's beliefs and attitudes, not a behavior caused by his drinking and/or drugging. For example, while heavy drinkers are often abusers, the majority of alcoholics are not.

Substance abuse does not cause men to be abusive or violent, but it can trigger abuse and/or increase its level and frequency if a man is already abusive. This often happens in one or more of the following ways:

- An abuser's belief that a substance will make him more aggressive becomes a self-fulfilling prophesy. He believes he can control others, so he takes action to control them.

- Substances may make a man more likely to misunderstand his partner's behavior and interpret her motives incorrectly, increasing his belief that violence is justified.

Domestic Abuse and Substance Abuse

I have the right to control and dominate my partner.

Aggressive actions are legitimate tools of control.

Alcohol/drugs make aggressivness seem okay.

I am entitled to be aggressive when I am high.

I will not be held responsible if I am high.

- Substances increase a man's sense of personal power and domination, which makes it more likely that he will attempt to exercise power and control.

- Abusers may intentionally get high to give themselves an excuse for violence, or to numb any guilt they feel about it.

- Abusers may use their substance abuse as a justification for their partner abuse or as a way to disclaim responsibility: "The alcohol made me do it."

An analogy to a bush with thorns helps one understand the relationship between substance abuse and domestic abuse. A seed grows into a bush with big, obtrusive thorns. Water gets it started and fertilizer makes it grow bigger, faster, and stronger. Taking away some water and fertilizer might make it grow less, but it still has dangerous thorns.

Abuse works the same way. Substance abuse doesn't cause abusive behavior, but it may trigger it or make it worse. Dealing with alcohol and drug abuse—taking away the water and fertilizer—may reduce the frequency and intensity of violence for a while, but it doesn't end coercive control or stop the abuse for the long term.

Thus, alcohol and most drugs may trigger belligerent, aggressive, or violent behavior. Consider the following questions to assess the way alcohol and drugs affect your behavior.

- Do you use being high as an excuse for abuse or violence, or to make you feel less guilty about it?

- Do you blame your partner for your abuse and for problems caused by your substance abuse?

- Do you insist that only what you do while you're high counts as abusive?

- Are you still controlling and abusive when sober, even if you're only physically violent when high?

- Does your drinking or drugging make your partner afraid for her safety?

- Do most incidents of violence get more severe when you are drunk?

If you answer "yes" to any, certainly several, of these questions, then alcohol and drugs are making your abusive behavior worse and more damaging. And you are responsible for your behavior and for dealing with it.

Accept Your Responsibility

Being high is not an excuse or justification for abusive behavior, and does not absolve an abuser of responsibility for his actions. Sometimes men claim to "lose it," black out, or be unable to make conscious decisions because of the influence of drugs or alcohol. However, think about the man who gets drunk and beats his wife, but carefully avoids hitting her face so the injuries will not be seen. Or he throws things, but throws hers and not his. He never "loses control" when other people are around to observe his behavior. He can't remember what happened after a blackout, but he can remember the event and what he did to his partner. This man didn't lose control. He tried to use his drunkenness to justify his abuse.

Or think about the Mississippi legislator. He didn't get what he wanted, so he bloodied her nose. Even if the alcohol increased violence, he still would be responsible for his actions while intoxicated because he clearly made the conscious choice to use alcohol and get drunk.

Think about all those who drink, drive, and cause accidents. They are morally and legally responsible for their actions. Similarly, if you abuse another, you are responsible—even if you are under the influence of drugs or alcohol.

Deal with Your Abuse

Given the likelihood that substance use or abuse may cause domestic abuse to be worse or more frequent, one might expect that programs for dealing with one would also address the other. However, each of the issues is a complex problem requiring a range of responses, and each has different root causes. Consequently, domestic abuse and substance abuse programs often do not address the problems of the other, and many programs do not integrate domestic violence and substance abuse services. But you will need to deal with both.

Deal with Substance Abuse

Substance abuse interventions may be appropriate and needed in many cases involving domestic abuse, but those that focus on substance abuse are likely to deal only with the domestic abuse symptoms rather than the root cause of the abuse. Focus on substance abuse in cases of domestic abuse is like having a broken wrist and dealing with it by using painkillers. At best, they will only take away the symptoms. You'll need a different treatment to help your bones heal properly. Similarly, substance abuse treatment alone is not likely to reduce coercive control or domestic abuse over the long term, for the following reasons:

- Substance abuse programs generally do not address the cause of domestic abuse.

- Abusers are violent and controlling, whether or not they are under the influence of drugs or alcohol.

- People who want to quit drinking or drugging do not necessarily want to treat their partner better or give up control of them.

- Most domestic abusers do not choose to examine and change their entitlement attitudes during substance abuse treatment.

- Substance abuse treatment doesn't overcome the social pressure and training that supports the inappropriate control of women by men.

Thus, while treatment for substance abuse may be needed and important, it alone is not likely to address domestic abuse issues.

Deal with Domestic Abuse

If you have a domestic abuse problem—like the Mississippi legislator—you need to take responsibility for the real, basic reason you abuse others rather than just deal with the symptoms. Think again about the law maker. Is there any reason to believe that if he stopped drinking, he would stop abusing? Doubtful. In these cases, the root cause is not the alcohol. It is the man's abusive beliefs, expectations, and behavior. He probably needs to participate in a batters' intervention program that addresses such issues.

Deal with All Abuse

Substance abuse programs and domestic abuse programs typically do not address problems of the other type of abuse because the causes and social contexts are so different. However, it frequently is important to treat problems of substance abuse and domestic abuse at the same time if you are to create lasting changes in behavior and stop domestic abuse. This means that if you are enrolled in a domestic abuse program, and you have a drug or alcohol problem, you should consider enrolling in a substance abuse program at the same time (and vice versa).

Various substance abuse diagnostic, service, and treatment centers are available to help assess whether you have a problem with alcohol or drugs and whether you need help. The following questions should help you determine whether you should seek such assistance:

- Do you ever feel bad or guilty about your alcohol or drug use?

- Do your spouse, partner, children or other persons ever complain about your use of alcohol or drugs?

- When you're sober, do you sometimes regret things you did or said while drinking or using drugs?

- Has alcohol or drug use ever created problems between you and your spouse or others?

If you answer "yes" to any of these questions, you may need a more detailed understanding of your possible problems and whether you should seek additional help.

No single treatment is appropriate for everyone who needs help. The type of help you choose should depend on your own needs and how severe your struggle is. Programs might range from self-help support groups, to outpatient programs, to inpatient programs in the most severe cases. If your assessment suggests you might have a problem, find professional help in determining your next step.

Questions for Reflection or Group Study

1. Consider the four questions under the section, "Dealing with all abuse." Should you go to the website to help determine whether you have a problem with alcohol or drugs and whether you need help? Why do you conclude this?

2. Chapter 5 discussed four "unhealthy approaches" to responsibility, listed below. Give an example of how you often use each of these approaches in dealing with substance abuse.

   Denying

   Rationalizing

SUBSTANCE ABUSE

Minimizing

Blaming

3. Think about the difference between domestic abuse and substance abuse by placing an "x" in the column for the one that best fits the described behavior.

Possible Behavior	Domestic Abuse	Substance Abuse
1. Use being high as an excuse for abuse or violence, or to feel less guilty about it?		
2. Blame partner for any actions or problems preceded by drinking?		
3. Insist that only what is done while drunk or high counts as abusive?		
4. Are controlling and abusive, even if physically violent only when drunk?		
5. If one drinks or uses drugs, partner is afraid for her own safety?		
6. Most incidents of violence occur if and when drunk?		

SUBSTANCE ABUSE

4. Consider the pros and cons of participating in either of two types of programs by completing the form below. What conclusion do you reach?

When You Should Participate in a Drug/Alcohol Program	When You Should Participate in a Batterer Program
1.	1.
2.	2.
3.	3.

Personal Reflection

Which of the learning objectives for this chapter is most important to you in stopping abuse and transforming your life? Why?

CHAPTER 17
Abusive Communication

Learning Objectives

After completing this chapter, you should be able to:
- Distinguish between communication that is effective and that which is abusive.
- Understand how an abusive individual avoids communication or refuses to communicate in order to further his abuse and control.
- Describe the types of communication processes, both sending and receiving, verbal and nonverbal, that are used to control or hurt someone and are abusive.
- Explain how an abusive attitude can play out in abusive verbal messages, abusive nonverbal messages, and digital abuse that often combines the two.
- Discuss the effect on communication of failing to listen effectively and failing to learn.

THE 1967 FILM, *COOL HAND LUKE*, USED THE phrase, "What we've got here is failure to communicate," to describe heated exchanges between Luke, played by Paul Newman, and a prison warden. The phrase describes only part of the problem in matters of domestic violence and abuse. Failure to communicate no doubt contributes to bad domestic relationships, and good communication is an essential tool for forming caring, loving relationships. Beyond that, however, men often use communication techniques to abuse, hurt, and terrorize their partner, as their communication patterns are deeply rooted in their attitudes and beliefs that they may abuse their partner to get what they want.

About Communication

Communication is a "two-way street" that involves sending and receiving information. It may have several goals, such as solving problems or accomplishing tasks, creating a relationship between the people involved, or creating or maintaining a desired image of the ones doing the communicating.

Sending information involves much more than talking, writing, or simply exchanging words. In most cases, the actual words exchanged are a minor part of communication, and the nonverbal actions of the people involved are more important.

Listening is perhaps the most important aspect of communication. It is making a conscious effort to use the senses to take in information from others and understand—learn—what they are communicating. Learning is the process of gaining knowledge or skill through, among other things, listening.

Effective Communication

Effective communication involves one party sending information and another receiving it and learning or understanding what the sender wants or needs, how they feel, what they like or dislike, or other things one needs to respond to. If information isn't sent or received properly, people will not respond appropriately, and healthy, nonabusive conflict or other problems are likely to result.

Good communication helps solve problems or accomplish tasks; creates a relationship of respect, love, and peace; and communicates the best the parties have to offer. Communication can also have a dark side, and this dark side may involve verbal abuse, threats, and intimidation.

Abusive Communication

Abusive communication is particularly dangerous because it can start so little and become so big. It often starts with just a few, slightly unkind words and grows from there, to more hurtful words, intimidation, and threats. If abusers feel their verbal techniques are not working, they are likely to turn to physical abuse.

Abusive communication alone is not illegal, leaves no physical wounds or scars, and usually can be hidden or denied. You can roar at your partner, berate her, or belittle her into submission without being confronted or jailed. But it can cause your partner to feel worthless, and cause a cycle of self-blame, self-loathing, and alienation where she blames herself for how you treat her.

Abusive communication can play out in each of the four situations discussed below.

Abusive Verbal Messages

Using words as weapons is as old as human language. Sometimes they can be more powerful and abusive than fists. James 3:5–6 says:

> Likewise, the tongue is a small part of the body, but it makes great boasts. Consider what a great forest is set on fire by a small spark. The tongue also is a fire, a world of evil among the parts of the body. It corrupts the whole body, sets the whole course of one's life on fire, and is itself set on fire by hell.

Words are powerful. Sharp criticism and cruel taunts can hurt another person even more than physical violence. Unkind words cause fear, hopelessness, guilt, pain, and other negative emotions, and they injure spirits and devastate lives. Such words leave marks on the person's psyche, helping to form the picture the receiver holds of herself. If she repeatedly hears messages that she is worthless and ugly and idiotic, her subconscious will begin to believe that it is true. The words become imbedded in her mind, along with the pain that someone who should love her and cherish her apparently doesn't think very much of her at all.

Following are examples of the many ways you might use words to hurt, control, and abuse your partner:

- Accusing
- Blaming
- Criticizing, putting her down
- Threatening
- Insulting and ridiculing

- Name calling
- Swearing or being lewd
- Distorting what happened in an earlier interaction
- Using fighting words and phrases
- Misusing religious doctrines
- Using minimizing phrases or unflattering comparisons.

Abusive Nonverbal Messages

Although we usually think of communication in terms of words, nonverbal communication, often described as communication without words, is an indispensable part of interpersonal communication. Your actions speak louder than your words. Your partner, who is on the receiving end of abusive nonverbal messages, may say words that tend to mask the situation and suggest that she is okay, while her nonverbal messages show real fear.

Nonverbal communication includes behavior that is easily seen as well as less obvious. It is impossible to list all the types of nonverbal behavior, as there are so many and they are so complicated. The following are some common examples of nonverbal communication you might use to abuse others.

- Sulking
- Smirking, rolling eyes, contemptuous facial expressions
- Yelling, raising the voice
- Using angry expressions or gestures
- Demonstrating negative body language
- Flexing muscles or clenching fists
- Getting in partner's face
- Poking with a finger
- Refusing to respond—using the silent treatment

Digital Abuse

Technology bridges gaps, maintains connections, and makes information more accessible than ever before. But it also has a dark side. You can exploit it to monitor, control, shame, and intimidate your victim—to engage in digital abuse, that can be both verbal and nonverbal. It can cause profound damage to your victim's life beyond the obvious fear and emotional distress it causes.

Some important types of digital abuse are as follows:

- Digital Stalking: using smartphones, social media, video/audio recording or other devices to monitor, intimidate, and control the victim.

- Excessive Texting/Calling: bombarding victims with endless calls, texts, and other such communication. A victim may need to answer the phone on the first call or immediately read and respond to texts to avoid being punished.

- Monitoring/Control Over Social Media: requiring victims to provide total access to all their communications with others, preventing the victim from having social media accounts, or maintaining control over her digital activity, including landlines and mobile phones.

- Video/Audio Recording: using images, video, and audio as a way to control or punish your victim, regardless of whether or not the victim has granted permission to be recorded or photographed. Such recordings can also be used as leverage to shame the victim into giving in to your demands to prevent them from sharing the files with others.

- Revenge Pornography: It is a couple's right if they choose to record or photograph intimate acts. However, victims may be coerced or manipulated into doing so, and some may have no idea that they are being recorded. You might post intimate images of someone online to get back at them for something you didn't like, or share such images with others without your partner's knowledge as a way to punish or humiliate her or to threaten her if she does not give in to your demands.

ABUSIVE COMMUNICATION

Failing to Listen

Listening is usually considered to be the act of hearing a sound and understanding what you hear. More broadly, however, listening involves giving attention to both verbal and nonverbal communication for the purpose of learning what is being communicated. You concentrate on what you hear or see in order to understand the message and learn what the speaker is conveying.

Listening as not a simple, passive task. It requires more than just being quiet and allowing someone to talk while you remain silent and appear to absorb information from them. Listening is an active process that involves hearing and understanding the words that are being spoken, but also observing the tone of voice, the volume, and other nonverbal signals such as facial expressions and body language the sender is communicating. It also involves paying attention, thinking about what was said, and remembering the message.

Poor listening ultimately affects communication and relationships in two ways. First, if you are not receiving information, you can easily distort the message and prevent an accurate exchange of information and ideas.

Second, failing to listen effectively or not responding appropriately always tells the speaker something about how you see her and is likely to contribute to her low self-worth. When you ignore her, you are telling her that she isn't worth listening to. If you interrupt her, look angry while she is talking, or make snap judgments about what she is saying, you convey the message that she is stupid or uninformed. This upsets her, raises her stress level, and limits her ability to solve problems; and allows you to continue to control and hurt her.

Some bad listening habits are as follows:

- Intentionally ignoring what is being said.
- Faking attention while not listening.
- Changing topics for no apparent reason.
- Interrupting when the partner is speaking.
- Twisting her words.
- Not clarifying or responding.
- Calling the subject uninteresting.

- Listening only to her words and not observing her nonverbal signals.

- Tolerating or creating distractions.

- Rushing your partner and making her feel that she's wasting your time.

- Showing interest in something other than the conversation.

- Thinking about your response rather than listening.

- Getting ahead of your partner and finishing her thoughts.

- Saying, "Yes, but . . .," as if your mind is already made up.

Failing to Learn

Learning involves gaining knowledge or skill through schooling, study—or listening. Sometimes you hear what is being communicated but don't learn what the communication intended. All of us carry with us deeply ingrained assumptions or generalizations that are pictures in our heads of "how things are" and that influence how we understand the world, the people with whom we interact, and what we learn from certain communication. Unfortunately, you may hold deeply held feelings of entitlement that cause you to refuse to communicate, listen, and learn from your partner. The assumptions and beliefs in your head often are wrong, and frequently are different than the beliefs and assumptions held by your partner. Such notions are likely to create barriers that prevent you from really hearing what your partner is saying, or from learning what she is trying to convey. Some examples of assumptions and beliefs that can prevent true learning and cause you to hear what you believe, rather than believe what you hear, are:

- You have your own agenda that limits the issues that are open for discussion.

- You believe that listening suggests lack of authority or power.

- You are self-centered and think mainly about yourself.

- You have negative attitudes about women.

ABUSIVE COMMUNICATION

- You believe that just letting your partner talk is enough, and you don't need to respond.

- You react without thinking, and quickly begin judging, advising, moralizing, lecturing, ordering, threatening, or otherwise responding critically.

- You either disregard her emotions or let them win out over learning.

- Deeply held beliefs cause you to react negatively to hot-button words or actions that cause you to have an inappropriate emotional reaction.

Your beliefs and biases, the pictures in your mind, are there even when you do not sense them. They are powerful, and determine what you hear and learn and do. If they are inaccurate, as they often are, they will lead you to communicate badly, prevent you from learning from your partner, and often provide an excuse for your abusive behavior.

Questions for Reflection or Group Study

1. James 1:19 states, "My dear brothers and sisters, take note of this: Everyone should be quick to listen, slow to speak and slow to become angry." What does this suggest for you about communication?

2. Think of three examples of your partner feeling hurt in a communication where you said one thing and acted differently. Analyze each action by completing the following chart:

What Happened	The Verbal Message	The Nonverbal Message

ABUSIVE COMMUNICATION

3. What conclusion do you draw from these examples?

4. List three of the habits from the Failing to Listen section that you are most likely to be guilty of and indicate the effects of these habits on your partner.

Bad Listening Habits	Effects of the Bad Habits

5. What conclusions do you draw from this?

6. List three assumptions and beliefs (such as those listed in the Failure to Learn section), that you often carry in your head that affect your communication with your partner, and describe the effect of each.

Assumptions/Beliefs	Effects

Personal Reflection

Which of the learning objectives for this chapter is most important to you in stopping abuse and transforming your life? Why?

CHAPTER 18
Peaceful Communication

Learning Objectives

After completing this chapter, you should be able to:
- Use your intuition and what you know about communication to guide you to communicate peacefully.
- Listen to your partner and demonstrate that you care about her and what she says.
- Convey your whole messages clearly.
- Use I statements to convey unwanted messages.
- Address failures to communicate that occur notwithstanding your best efforts.

CHAPTER 17 INTRODUCED "COMMUNICATION" and explored its use as a tool of abuse. This chapter provides guidance for effective, peaceful, nonviolent, noncoercive communication. You can communicate effectively and with peace if you want to.

Avoid Abusive Communication

Communicating with your partner without becoming abusive is not difficult. You no doubt have a basic, intuitive understanding of language and communication practices that allows you to make choices between words and actions that communicate an abusive message and those that foster peace. Even if you grew up in a troubled environment with poor role models, you were no doubt exposed from a young age to the basics of how to communicate "appropriately" in normal social situations. Just like you know the color blue when you see it, within a practical range you know what communication is hurtful and what isn't, what is peaceful and what isn't. You know, for example, that profanity and ridicule are hurtful, that yelling and clenching a fist can be threatening, and that silence can communicate as well as words. And you know which words and actions are supportive and comforting, and which are not.

You probably have at times chosen to use communication as a tool of abuse. But you have the ability to use language and nonverbal communication that is peaceful if you want to. You have the power to stop the hurt by changing the way you communicate. Different situations call for different approaches, but your basic understanding and intuition will guide you to a passing grade in any of them. Do what you know is right, behave as you know you should, and your communication will not be abusive. Perhaps it could be better and more effective, but it won't be abusive.

Listen with Empathy

Most of us—and certainly men who abuse women—refuse to listen or don't listen well. Review the Failing to Listen section of the previous chapter to remind you of some of the ways you may fail to listen. Over time the result of such failure to listen is that you feed your worst abusive impulses, never really understand your partner's needs or concerns, and set the stage for continuing domestic difficulties and abuse.

Listening effectively to your partner is your best opportunity to receive information, learn from her, really know her, know what is going on in her life—and convey your love and respect to her. Really listening requires you to do much more than just be quiet and allow her to talk. It requires you to (1) receive the information she is conveying and (2) demonstrate that you care about her and what she says. When she talks, you need to suspend your judgment, be patient, and put yourself in her shoes—empathize with her—to accurately perceive the meaning of her spoken words and grasp the nonverbal signals she conveys. Some important skills for accomplishing these objectives are discussed below.

Listen to Yourself

Remember that the beliefs and assumptions in your head often prevent you from listening and learning, and they may cause you to hear what you want to hear and fit "reality" and "truth" to your own needs and wants.

These beliefs and assumptions, along with the pressure of current issues in your life, may create filters that prevent you from paying attention to what your partner says. They tend to limit you to familiar ways of thinking and therefore often shape what you hear others say to conform to what you expect or want them to say. You hear what you believe, rather than believe what you hear.

To set the stage for effective listening, try to understand yourself, see the filters through which you listen, and make adjustments if these filters are leading you astray. Critically examine and understand yourself, and separate your feelings, personal agendas, biases, and beliefs from what your partner is communicating. Look objectively at what is going on in your world, be receptive to new information and ideas, and make a conscious decision that you will listen carefully to your partner, no matter what your beliefs and assumptions are or what is going on in your life.

Listen with the Right Attitude

Your attitude will affect what you hear, as well as how your partner feels about and responds to your reactions to her. If you feel superior, all-powerful, angry, or otherwise have a negative attitude, you are almost sure to respond to her communication in a way that reflects your attitude. On the other hand, if you have a positive attitude and are interested and engaged, you will hear what she says and through your response communicate that she is valuable and important.

To convey a positive attitude and avoid a negative one, show through your love, patience, and attention that you care about your partner and her situation.

Capture the Nonverbal and Verbal Messages

Your partner communicates a great deal more than she says in words, through various nonverbal actions such as tone, body language, and expressions. To listen effectively to her you need to observe her carefully and "hear" both the verbal and nonverbal messages.

Some of the more common, often problematic, nonverbal messages involve emotions such as nervousness, defensiveness, frustration, and anger. When your partner is speaking, carefully observe her and the emotions she reveals. Consider them as valuable information about what she is communicating.

Sometimes what you see will be different from what you are hearing. For example, her words may say she is okay while her body language conveys that she isn't, and you need to be aware of how your manipulation is affecting her. When this is the case, the nonverbal communication is more likely to be accurate, as people are better able to control what they say than how they look or what they do. Therefore, you often should believe what you see rather than what you hear—although, this does not mean you get to decide how she is feeling. If her message seems conflicting, you may need to explore matters more deeply, or perhaps defer the conversation.

Offer Feedback

Providing feedback keeps you actively involved in the conversation and lets your partner know her message is being received. You can provide verbal feedback by reacting to what she says, repeating it back to her in slightly different words, acknowledging her feelings and emotions, and sincerely answering her questions. Asking sincere questions at the right time is an important way of providing feedback. Appropriate questions not only get information, but also show that you are listening, care enough to seek additional information, and believe that your partner has value.

Improve Your Message

You need to convey messages in a way that builds up your partner and makes your communication nonabusive and noncoercive, as well as more effective and helpful. The following sections suggest skills you can use to accomplish this.

Communicate by Listening

As discussed in more detail in the previous chapter, how you listen and receive information is an important way of sending your message. Failing to listen effectively or not responding tells the speaker something about how you view her. When you ignore her, you are telling her that she isn't worth listening to. If you interrupt her, look angry while she is talking, or make snap judgments about what she is saying, you convey the message that she is stupid or uninformed. On the other hand, listening carefully to everything your partner communicates conveys the idea that she is valuable and worth listening to, and tends to validate her as an important human being.

Convey a Whole Message

Effective communication requires several types of expression, such as conveying information, sharing thoughts, and expressing feelings and emotions. Leaving one or more out or having conflicting expressions creates confusion and distrust, as your partner will not receive what she needs to hear and will sense that you are withholding a part of the message or being dishonest.

For example, she will have trouble accepting your beliefs if she doesn't know the information on which they are based, or if they are inconsistent, or if they have led to actions that are controlling and abusive. She cannot empathize with your feelings if you don't tell her what they are or why you have them. Thus, you need to be especially careful to accurately and completely share the facts you want to communicate, clearly tell her what you believe based on those facts, and honestly express any feelings or emotions you have about the situation. However, remember that this sharing of the whole message does not give you permission to use your communication as a tool for further abuse. The key is to communicate a whole message without being abusive or threatening.

State Your Message Clearly

Communication often is comprised of vague statements that don't address real issues or needs, raise questions rather than make statements, express anger or other emotions, attempt to manipulate, or present other problems. To communicate effectively you need to:

- Use positive statements to say clearly and simply what you intend. This often means addressing one issue at a time while speaking slowly and deliberately without in any way threatening or intimidating.

- Address specific issues so both of you will know exactly what you are talking about.

- Support your verbal with your nonverbal communication. Make eye contact, demonstrate your sincerity, and use a tone of voice that conveys your intent.

- Support your partner without detracting from the conversation. This may involve recognizing her viewpoint, telling her if you agree with her, or finding other ways of confirming her and making her feel valued.

Avoid Negative Communication

Certain types of messages will nearly always result in reactions that are negative and demonstrate defensiveness, resentment, anger, sadness, aggression, or other negative emotions. When this happens, your partner is not likely to hear and will almost surely react with fear or simply shut down. The following are some of the types of messages you may send that create negative reactions, and that generally need to be avoided.

- Criticizing—finding fault, blaming, or making negative evaluations about your partner.

- Insincere praising—evaluating your partner as a gimmick to manipulate her.

- Diagnosing—telling your partner why she does what she does.

- Advising or being overly opinionated—telling your partner what she ought to do.

- Moralizing or preaching—claiming social, moral, or theological authority.

- Generalizing—telling her "you always" or "you never."

- Labeling—using simple descriptions to describe some aspect of your partner.

- Ordering—trying to use your power to get compliance.

- Interrupting—"butting in" when she speaks, particularly in public.

- Threatening—emphasizing the punishment that will result if your partner does not comply.

- Blaming—finding fault with your partner or holding her responsible for your actions.

Handle Failure to Communicate

Chapter 17 began with Luke noting, "What we've got here is failure to communicate." Similarly, even if you believe you have avoided abusive communication and used the ideas and techniques outlined above, you may feel you still have a failure to communicate. Notwithstanding your best efforts, tension and misunderstandings still exist. The problem you were hoping to solve is still a problem. You have not received the response you expected and hoped for. Four ideas for dealing with this kind of situation are outlined below.

Review Your Expectations

If you are thinking your communication process failed, first look closely at what you hoped to accomplish with the communication. Was your purpose to have an honest exchange of ideas and information, or was it to convince your partner to do what you want her to do—to continue to control her? Did you want a good relationships or did you want to be right? Is the problem a lack of understanding, or that you don't like what she says and does?

In summary, you may have engaged in the best of communication processes, and still be wrong, fail to control your partner, and not like her response. You may be experiencing a failure to control and get what you want rather than a "failure to communicate."

We discussed in Chapter 15 that anger doesn't cause abuse, but is an effect of an abusive attitude. Similarly, what appears to be a failure to communicate is often a consequence of an abusive attitude. Remember that effective communication is not a tool to manipulate or change others, and using it for that purpose destroys its effectiveness. In our context, its purpose is to share information and ideas, solve problems, and improve relationships.

Review the preceding sections of this chapter and the section in Chapter 2 on "dialogue" to help you decide whether your true purpose was to communicate, or to convince and control. Think deeply about whether the problem is poor communication or your abusive actions. And aim to correct what needs to be corrected.

Look at Yourself

Effective communication requires trust. For you to effectively communicate with a partner, you need to demonstrate trustworthiness—that what you say is true and that you will do what you say you will do. But victims of abuse do not trust their abusers—who have so often violated their ability to trust and by their own behavior made establishing trust so very difficult or impossible.

For you to begin to build the trust required for effective communication, you need to fundamentally change your consciousness, beliefs, and behavior, and stop the abuse, along the lines discussed in Chapter 4. You must honestly look deeply within yourself and find that you have accepted responsibility for your actions, been accountable for them, and made amends to the extent possible—along with other actions outlined in Part Two of this book. You should behave in ways that maintain peace, considering the discussion in Part Three, and in particular the chapters on Trust and Work With Your Partner.

If you are willing to learn these skills and apply them in your everyday life and interactions, you can work toward developing the trust that is needed for a level of communication that fundamentally alters how you interacts with those closest to you, including those you have hurt. You can go a long way toward avoiding a failure to communicate, and fix it when it does happen.

Empathize—More

In Chapter 6 we stated that empathy toward others is probably the most fundamental characteristic you need for dealing with your responsibility toward them and transforming your life. We noted earlier in this chapter, that to communicate effectively, you need to suspend your judgment, be patient, and put yourself in your partner's shoes—empathize with her—to accurately understand the meaning of her spoken words and grasp the nonverbal signals she conveys. In both of these cases, our suggestion involved walking in your partner's shoes, and appreciating her life as she lives it on a day-to-day basis as part of your effort to transform your life.

Empathy is also important in understanding problems with communication and improving the process. The act of empathy requires a level of deliberate, conscious, and calculated decision making about the act of communication. Walking in her shoes will help inform you of her perspective as to how to best communicate, and why your communication may have failed. Empathy will help you notice your interconnectedness and respect how your partner's needs impact your communication.

When you see the world from your partner's perspective, you are able to adapt your communication to what will be most effective for the relationship between the two of you. You can make purposeful decisions about how you communicate based on the perspective of your partner. This tends to reduce the likelihood of the communication failing, and helps you fix it if it fails by following the suggestions outlined earlier in this chapter.

Listen to the Context

Communication is more about listening than talking. We noted earlier that listening effectively and with empathy to your partner is your best opportunity to effectively communicate and avoid failed communication. However, we often listen only to the words said and gestures offered in the actual communication event, and in doing so, miss out on the context—the background facts and circumstances that give meaning to the actual communication.

Context tells you what importance to place on something, what assumptions to draw (or not) about what is being communicated, and puts meaning into the message. It deepens your understanding of the message so that true dialogue can take place. Context is especially important where abuse is a factor, and your partner is likely to be affected by worry, fear, distrust, and other emotions that make effective communication more difficult.

Listening to the context of what your partner is saying:

- Helps you understand what you're hearing.

- Helps you think about what might be done in response to what you hear.

- Inclines you to serve those with whom you are communicating, rather than seek to persuade them to do something you want.

- Helps you work on solving the right problem.

- Helps you recognize patterns developing with communication and relationship with your partner.

If you are concerned that your communication has failed, consider the context and try to respond to the entire picture.

Summary

You can build peace with your communication if you want to and make the effort to really listen effectively and convey your messages positively. A good test is to simply follow the Golden Rule of Matthew 7:12, "So in everything, do to others what you would have them do to you, for this sums up the Law and the Prophets." If you accept this biblical teaching, you will communicate with your partner in the same way you want her and others to communicate with you.

Questions for Reflection or Group Study

1. List several things you can do to help you communicate better and avoid using communication as a tool of abuse?

2. What message does the way you listen usually send to your partner?

3. List two things you can do to improve your listening skills. Why do you list these?

4. Complete the following chart by listing examples of three messages you have sent, either verbally or nonverbally, that created negative reactions by your partner.

Example of Message Causing Negative Reaction	Effect on Partner	Better Message

5. List three things you need to continue doing and to stop doing to foster more peaceful communication.

Continue Doing	Stop Doing

6. What is the most common reason you "fail to communicate?" What should you do about it?

7. Matthew 7:12 reads, "So in everything, do to others what you would have them do to you, for this sums up the Law and the Prophets." What does this suggest to you about how you should communicate?

> **Personal Reflection**
>
> Which of the learning objectives for this chapter is most important to you in stopping abuse and transforming your life? Why?

CHAPTER 19
Sexual Abuse

Learning Objectives

After completing this chapter, you should be able to:
- Explain the deeply held attitudes, beliefs, entitlements, and societal enforcements that contribute to sexual abuse.
- Understand and explain the traumatic effects of sexual abuse on victims.
- Explain the difference between consent and compliance, and judge when your partner has consented to sexual activity.
- Describe six types of sexual abuse and explain why all sexual abuse is wrong and is a violation of God's law, a woman's human rights, and often a violation of criminal law.

SUE WAS EIGHTEEN WHEN SHE MARRIED Carlos, who was twenty-two. For the first year of their marriage, Sue and Carlos had no significant problems, although occasionally Sue became quite uncomfortable when Carlos griped about her appearance, pressured her to wear clothes she didn't like, told jokes of a sexual nature, or otherwise raised sexual issues at just the wrong time. He occasionally touched and fondled her in ways and at times that she felt were highly inappropriate and caused her embarrassment, but most things seemed more or less normal. Then a pattern developed. When Sue was not as sexually responsive as Carlos wanted, he would pout and withdraw. Then sometimes he taunted her by calling her "frigid" or "lesbian" if she was not ready when called. Or sometimes he threatened infidelity: "If you won't have sex with me, then I will find it elsewhere."

On a few occasions, Carlos simply refused to accept "no" until Sue gave in to the pressure and had sex that was physically forced and clearly against her will, but that Sue did not resist to the point of a more physical altercation. Then one night Carlos returned home after a night of drinking with friends and began asking Sue for sex. This time Sue refused, in spite of increasing pressure and more aggressive tactics from Carlos. When she told Carlos "no" several times, more positively than usual, he knocked her down from the edge of the bed, held her down to the floor, slapped her hard across the face, and forcefully had sex with her, even though she was crying, telling him to stop and get off.

Their marriage came to be characterized by cycles of arguments that Carlos used as an excuse to force Sue to have sex. While actual physical altercations were rare, Sue often gave in because of her fear of what would happen if she didn't. He tried to justify his actions by saying things like "You are my wife, you can't say no" and claiming he loved her but she made him feel hurt, angry, disrespected, and sad.

Carlos sometimes even tried to use his perverted view of Scripture to justify his actions, claiming that Sue's body was not her own but was his. He claimed that as head of the household, he had a right to her body when it pleased him. He put down her faith and expressed doubt that she was a Christian, because a Christian wife, he claimed, would never turn down her husband.

Often Carlos was extremely apologetic after the fact. He would ask for her forgiveness, claim he loved her and would never hurt her intentionally, send her flowers, and promise never to do such a thing again.

Carlos's abuse involved physical, verbal, emotional, and sexual abuse. All are unacceptable. However, this chapter will focus on abuse of a sexual nature. It will set the stage for Chapter 20, which will discuss ideas for transforming one's life to one focused on sexual respect—respect that plays out in various ways, but at its core involves husbands and wives loving one another and treating one another accordingly.

Background

Questions of sexual ethics can cover a broad range of activities, and different individuals and different religious traditions often have different views as to what is right and wrong, acceptable or unacceptable, or what is a "sin." For example, questions relating to consensual activity involving homosexuality, sex outside marriage, sex not relating to procreation, etc.—questions involving who is doing what with whom—can be very controversial. This book will not address such activities that occur between free, consenting adults. Instead, it will focus on activities of a sexual nature that raise issues of power, consent, or choice, and may be abusive.

Some have advocated the mistaken notion that sexual abuse cannot occur within a relationship or a marriage, because a woman's being in such a relationship indicates that she desires to take part in sexual activities. Such view was generally endorsed by our legal system for roughly two centuries, and for many years in Western society a man could not be legally convicted of raping his wife. A married man was seen to have certain rights over his wife, and sex was generally among them. Such thinking dates back to Englishman Sir Matthew Hale, who wrote in 1736, "But the husband cannot be guilty of a rape committed by himself upon his lawful wife, for by their mutual matrimonial consent and contract the wife hath given herself up in this kind unto her husband which she cannot retract."[11]

Until the 1970s, various criminal jurisdictions in the United States defined rape as "forced sexual intercourse with a woman who is not his wife." Regrettably, viewing women as sex objects rather than valuable human beings is not uncommon today. Two influences cause and perpetuate such beliefs.

The Bible

Certain interpretations of the Bible unfortunately have led to the mistaken view that sexual abuse cannot occur within a serious relationship or a marriage. Scripture contains few direct references to sexual abuse or violence, and references that do exist—often Old Testament stories such as those of Joseph and Potiphar's wife (Genesis 39:1–23), the Levite and the concubine (Judges 19:11–30), and the rape of Tamar (II Samuel 13), have been interpreted in confusing and contradictory ways. In Biblical stories women frequently seem to be treated as property rather than human beings, the victims (women) rather than the perpetrators seem to be blamed, and sexual activity is confused with sexual violence, all leading some to interpretations that fail to condemn sexual abuse.

Biblical interpretations often have emphasized the form of sexual activity, i.e., who (gender, orientation), what (for procreation or not), and when (before or after marriage), and given almost no emphasis to the relationship between the two persons, and the presence or absence of power, consent, and mutuality. For example, some interpreters have concluded that while sexual activity outside of marriage is wrong, sexual activity inside of marriage is acceptable no matter what the circumstances and even if that activity is coercive and abusive rather than consensual and respectful. In this and the following chapters we will see how wrong this view is.

The Media

The media has contributed to development of a cultural and social environment that seems to condone unwanted sexual activity, and even sexual assault and violence against women. For example, magazines with photoshopped images of beautiful women are often thought to be largely responsible for causing problems relating to body image in many women and young girls by setting beauty standards—very thin, young, attractive woman expected to be sexy, sexually available, sexually submissive, and desirable—that are far from realistic. Television, often through advertisements that appear to present pornographic scenes, teaches that sex is something to be consumed and to which men are entitled. This leads to the mistaken view that, because sex is something that can be bought and sold, taking it by force is theft, not a personal violation, and taking it without consent becomes less morally reprehensible than other violent crimes. Movies frequently show scenes of violent and forceful sexual situations that seem to encourage the association of masculinity with violence, dominance, and power; and condone sexual assault.

All combined, this accumulation of influences perpetuates the mistaken idea that women are sexual objects, and that sexual objectification is simply a fact of life. At worst, it leads to what has been called a "rape culture," where violence against women, even rape, comes to be condoned to the point that it may be considered almost normal.

The fact is, however, that regardless of the cause, sexual abuse in any form is wrong—a violation of God's law, a woman's human rights, and often a violation of criminal law.

Sexual Abuse and Consent

Sexual abuse is commonly described as the use of the sexual relationship to fulfill the abusers need for control. It includes various forms of inappropriate and harmful actions, including innuendo and jokes based on gender or sexuality, repeated comments of a sexual nature, requests for sexual favors which make an individual uncomfortable and imply that rejection of this behavior will lead to negative consequences, unwelcome sexual advances up to use of physical force, and other types of sexual assault. It can be verbal, physical, or any act that forces a person to join in unwanted sexual activity or attention.

Regardless of the form, all forms of sexual abuse have one important thing in common: they are done without the consent of your victim.

Consent means your partner actively agrees with your actions and, without any coercion or pressure, agrees to participate. It is not that she is just willing to comply with your desires. Asking for consent and receiving your partner's response involves setting your personal boundaries and respecting those of your partner. If your partner consents, it lets you know that what you are doing is okay and wanted. If your partner does not consent, your actions of a sexual nature are against her will, are inappropriate, and are a form of abuse.

Both people must agree to an action or activity—every single time—for it to be with consent and consensual. Some characteristics of consent are:

- Consent must be voluntary, given without pressure or manipulation, and without fear arising from past violence and coercive behavior.

- Consent must be clearly communicated and informed. People who are drunk, high, or passed out can't consent to sexual activity.

- Your partner can consent only if she has the full story and understands what you will do.

- Consent must be active and affirmative. Silence is not consent.

- Consent is never implied by things like your partner's past behavior or what she wears.

- Your partner can change her mind—and say stop or things like "this doesn't feel good," "I don't like this," etc., which all indicate she has changed her mind without using that specific word—anytime she wishes.

- A person younger than the age of consent cannot consent.

In summary, all sexual activity should be mutual and agreeable to those involved. Without consent, in is never mutual. It is abusive.

Sexually Abusive Behavior

As we see in the case of Sue and Carlos, sexual abuse often starts with inappropriate behavior that has been normalized in our culture and is not an arrestable offense, and quickly escalates. Carlos's lack of sexual respect started to show itself with behavior that was not violent, but that resulted in a hostile home environment, and escalated to include a continuum of abusive actions, ultimately culminating in intimate partner rape. A continuum of different kinds of unacceptable sexually abusive behavior, all too common among abusive men, is illustrated as follows:

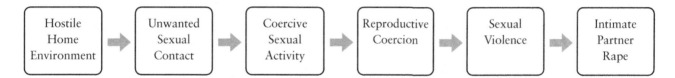

All such behavior is a serious violation, of God's law and the victim's human rights, and may violate criminal law. Some involves violence, but much occurs without the use of force: for example, manipulation, guilt, inducing one's partner to use different substances with the goal of sexual activity, shame, etc., create a hostile home environment and are unwanted, but not violent. How a victim responds to these types of violations is also important. Because she is silent, still, or is not screaming does not mean she is consenting to what is happening.

The following discusses each type in more detail.

Hostile Home Environment

Carlos's abuse started with a hostile home environment—not physically abusive, but not acceptable; not greatly different from other types of verbal, emotional, and psychological abuse. A hostile home environment like Sue experienced beginning with her second year of marriage is an environment that is not violent and doesn't involve unwanted physical contact, but that unreasonably interferes with family members' sense of safety and well-being, or creates an intimidating, hostile, or offensive home atmosphere. Actions that create a hostile home environment might not be criminal acts, but they generally violate the partner's human rights and God's law. Examples involving sexual abuse include actions such as:

- Laughing at or telling jokes that make fun of rape or other sexual violence.

- Calling your partner negative sexual names, such as bitch, cunt, whore, or slut.

- Saying such names in front of the kids.

- Judging women, and your partner, by their appearance.

- Making degrading comments about your partner's appearance.

- Pressuring your partner to wear clothes she doesn't want to wear.

- Accusing your partner of having affairs, flirting, or coming on to other men.

- Comparing her body to other women.

- Making her beg or feel cheap or dirty if she wants sex.

- Blaming her if you don't feel satisfied.

Although these types of actions have a sexual basis, at their core they involve verbal, psychological, and emotional abuse similar to that in other types of abusive actions. Such behavior, all unacceptable, is addressed in other chapters.

Unwanted Sexual Contact

Unwanted sexual contact involves actual physical contact, short of intercourse, in sexual situations where a man has an attitude of entitlement over his partner, but also knows or has reason to know that she doesn't want the contact. Unwanted sexual contact can occur at anytime and under any circumstance. It often happens as part of "routine" family or social situations, perhaps when drugs and alcohol are involved, sometimes in what otherwise might be seen as a romantic encounter, especially when the abusive individual feels a deep entitlement to his partner's body. Such contact might include:

- Touching in a way that may make your partner feel uncomfortable.

- Patting, groping, grabbing, or feeling.
- Kissing that is unwanted and out of context.

Such contact is abusive, fails to treat the woman as a valuable human being, and is a violation of God's law.

Coercive Sexual Activity

Coercive sexual activity is behavior intended to induce a woman to participate in a sexual activity, including intercourse, against her will, regardless of whether or not it happens. Such coercion often results from perceived gender roles or unequal distribution of resources, such as income, education, and employment, that lead men to feel entitled to control their partner and their sexual activity. The coercion involves repeated, ongoing, intentional control tactics used to get the woman to comply with a man's wishes in the sexual relationship. You refuse to accept "no." If the woman complies, it is still coercion. It might include behavior such as:

- Pouting, withdrawing, or sulking if denied a sexual request.
- Withholding affection if she doesn't want sex when you do.
- Begging her or pressuring her for sex.
- Imposing sexual acts when she is incapable of giving consent, such as when she is drunk or asleep.
- Making her feel guilty if she doesn't want sex when you do.
- Acting suspicious or questioning your relationship.
- Threatening to have sex with others or justifying promiscuity.
- Using pornography in ways that diminish her and portray women as objects rather than human beings.
- Intentionally withholding STD/STI/HIV/AIDS status.

Such activity by a man is clearly abusive.

Reproductive Coercion

Reproductive coercion is present when a man tries to exercise power and control over his partner to impregnate her against her will, control outcomes of a pregnancy, coerce her to have unprotected sex, interfere with contraceptive methods, or otherwise interfere with his partner's contraception use and pregnancy. One woman—let's call her Hellen—described her experience as follows:

> I had been seeing this guy for just over three months. One night he wanted to make love and I asked him to put on a condom. He said he didn't have one. I asked him to stop, and he wouldn't. And he said that it didn't matter, not to worry about it. At first, I sort of laughed cause I thought he was joking, but then I realized he was serious and I got scared. I told him to stop but he wouldn't, and I pushed him away but he pushed me back and pinned me down with his body. He was very strong. He raped me.[12]

Examples of reproductive coercion include:

- Forcing sex without a condom or not allowing other prophylaxis use.

- Hiding, withholding, or destroying a partner's contraceptives.

- Breaking or poking holes in a condom on purpose or removing a condom during sex.

- Not withdrawing when that was the agreed upon method of contraception.

- Threatening to hurt a partner who does not agree to become pregnant.

- Forcing a partner to carry a pregnancy to term against her wishes through threats or acts of violence.

- Forcing a female partner to terminate a pregnancy when she does not want to.

- Injuring a female partner in a way that may cause a miscarriage.

- Lying, pressuring, or manipulating a partner involving a sexual act.

Reproductive coercion has devastating consequences, including unintended pregnancy, abortion, and psychological trauma. It often is a violation of criminal law, and always is a violation of God's law and the victim's rights.

Sexual Violence

Sexual abuse involving forceful, unwanted actions and violent sexual assaults is clearly a criminal act. Such abuse occurs when an individual forces his partner to take part in sexual activity without consent. An individual who is responsible for subjecting his partner to sexual abuse may use threats, coercion, or violence in order to force his spouse to take part in sexual activities. Some specific examples might include:[13]

- Forcing sex through physical pressure or assault.
- Forcing sex through threats and fear.
- Inserting objects into your partner's vagina against her will.
- Forcing her to have sex with other men or women.
- Forcing her into sex trafficking.
- Coercing sex in a way she doesn't want.
- Intimate partner rape.

Intimate partner rape is one among several forms of sexual violence. However, given the view among some men that providing sex is a woman's obligation—a view often fostered by erroneous religious beliefs—it will be given special attention.

The definition of rape is very simple: "the crime, typically committed by a man, of forcing another person to have sexual intercourse with the offender against their will." Notice that "against their will" includes not only forcing intercourse through physical pressure or assault, but also forcing it through threats, fear, or other intimidating actions, or when the partner is incapable of giving her consent.

Research is clear that rape has major physical and psychological consequences on the victim. Sometimes women are hit, kicked, or burned during sex, and may suffer black eyes, broken bones, blood clots in their heads or knife wounds when rape follows physical assaults. Most suffer major pain and often bleeding during and after a partner's assault, miscarriages and stillbirths, unwanted pregnancies, and continuing pelvic pain and painful intercourse. Psychological consequences of rape include anxiety, depression, sleep disturbances, eating disorders, lack of interest in sex, fear of men, other social phobias, substance abuse, suicidal ideas, and PTSD.[14]

Victims of intimate partner rape appear to be just as likely, or more likely, to experience such outcomes as victims of stranger rape. A wife rape victim experiences the violation of her body in a place (usually her home) and by a person previously "deemed safe." Living with a person who has sexually assaulted her means there is no place in which she may feel safe from future assaults. Such an experience may cause her to cease believing that she is secure in the world, that the world has order and meaning, and that she is a worthy person.

Notwithstanding the view of some, a man is raping his intimate partner if he commits sexual acts without her consent and/or against her will. Intimate-partner rapists rape to reinforce their power or control over their partners or families, rather than as a sexual act. Such acts may be committed through physical force, threats of force, or as a result of fear arising from past attacks. A partner does not need to "put up a good fight," and beliefs such as: "women enjoy forced sex," "women say no when they really mean yes, "or "it's a wife's duty to have sex" are simply wrong and unacceptable, and not a defense against the crime of rape or any form of sexual abuse.

Such acts are a crime in all fifty states. Most states charge the crime in the same way that rape between strangers would be handled, and penalize marital rape like any other rape, with fines that may exceed $50,000 and prison terms that vary between several years and life in prison without parole. The applicable punishment generally varies according to the severity of the circumstances of the crime.

SEXUAL ABUSE

Questions for Reflection or Group Study

1. Review the story of Sue and Carlos. List the things Carlos did that were abusive.

2. Discuss three situations where what you might claim is consent, is compliance and not consent.

3. Provide examples of actions that fit in each of the following types of sexual abuse.

   Hostile home environment:

   Unwanted sexual contact:

   Coercive sexual activity:

   Reproductive coercion:

Sexual violence:

Intimate partner rape:

4. What do your answers to questions 1–3 tell you about your true beliefs relating to sexual matters and how they affect your partner?

5. What are some consequences of sexual abuse?

> ## Personal Reflection
>
> Which of the learning objectives for this chapter is most important to you in stopping abuse and transforming your life? Why?

CHAPTER 20
Sexual Respect

Learning Objectives

After completing this chapter, you should be able to:
- Understand that all sexual activity must be mutually agreed, based on respect and trust, and that coercive actions to gain compliance are not acceptable.
- Accept that all sexual activity should take place in an environment of respect, caring, equal regard for one another, mutuality, and equality.
- Change your beliefs about sexuality in order to change your behavior toward your partner.
- Understand that insisting an abused partner forgive you or reconcile with you is abusive, and a continuation of the original abuse.
- Deal effectively with issues of forgiveness and reconciliation relating to sexual abuse and respect.

THINK AGAIN ABOUT CARLOS AND SUE, INTRO-
duced in Chapter 19. Carlos's abusive behavior demonstrated a particularly personal and bad form of domestic abuse that included a range of inappropriate or illegal sexual activities, from things he did to create a hostile home environment to violence. Carlos needs to quit the abuse and accept that all sexual activity must be mutually agreed, based on respect and trust.

Sue has been hurt so badly that she may never feel safe again in their relationship, and almost surely will not consent to sexual activity until some level of trust is established. Carlos needs to make choices that are not threatening and that are intended to foster that trust. His movement from sexual abuse to sexual respect will need to include changes in behavior based on most of the principles discussed in other chapters of this book: changes that will transform his life.

About Sexual Respect

If you have been sexually abusive, you need to transform your life and become sexually respectful. In particular, sexual respect includes exhibiting the following attitudes, beliefs, and behaviors regarding your intimate partner, which we assume to be a woman:

- Be honest with her.

- Be trustworthy and loyal to her.

- Recognize that all sexual activity must be agreed and mutual, with her specific consent as explained in Chapter 19. Any activity that is not agreeable to both is without consent and is sexual abuse.

- Treat all sexual activity as private and confidential. Do not "kiss and tell."

- Be monogamous in your relationship. Just one woman.

Such respect is characterized as love in Ephesians 5. Verse 33 states, "However, each one of you also must love his wife as he loves himself, and the wife must respect her husband." Men who love their wives, or those with whom they have an intimate relationship, as much as they love themselves will not use this scripture as a tool for demanding respect. Instead they will care for their partners with the same concern they show for maintaining their own interests. They will devote their time, money, desires, etc. to their partner. Such examples of love will demonstrate respect for her, and may earn her respect in return.

Sexual respect is the opposite of "male entitlement" or "male privilege:" the belief that men are tough and strong and aggressive and have an inherent right to power over their intimate partners. Sexual respect means a man is not *entitled* to have sex with a partner, to treat the partner with contempt or scorn, to use physical force against her, or to engage in emotional manipulation.

As noted above, sexual respect involves behavior consistent with the principles discussed in other chapters of this book, such as responsibility, accountability, confession, restitution, and various aspects of maintaining peace. However, it involves special issues relating to repentance, forgiveness, and reconciliation, discussed below.

Sexual Respect and Repentance

As discussed in more detail in Chapter 4, repentance is a transformation in which your fundamental character and being, including beliefs, feelings, and attitudes as well as behavior, become permanently different. In the case of sexual abuse, many of men's beliefs are flat out wrong and lead to abusive behavior. If you have been sexually abusive, you need to drastically and permanently change both.

Change Your Beliefs

Most of your beliefs about sexuality have been formed through observing your parents and parent figures, from media sources that dictate what is attractive and sexy—such as books, television, movies, the internet, or pornography—and/or through distorted views of biblical teaching. Often, the influences combine to reinforce male entitlement and lead men to believe that controlling and dominating a woman, particularly through sexual activity in marriage, is okay, or at least not too bad.

Men who feel entitled often express beliefs that sex is their right in marriage, wives have a "wifely duty" to make sex available, and a woman's refusal of sex is unfair or a control tactic. Under this belief system, women are perceived not as human beings with their own desires and feelings, but rather as objects and manipulators. Sexual abuse in various forms, from manipulation and pressure to rape, is viewed as justified. Not surprisingly, such beliefs often lead to sexual violence involving power, control, dominance and humiliation—and sometimes even murder, as the perpetrator believes that abuse is acceptable, justified, and unlikely to be reported.

All right-thinking people agree that actions consistent with such beliefs are a violation of the partner's human rights and God's law, and many violate criminal law as well. Any man who holds such beliefs needs to change them, as Jesus explained in rather interesting language in Matthew 23:25–26:

> Woe to you, teachers of the law and Pharisees, you hypocrites! You clean the outside of the cup and dish, but inside they are full of greed and self-indulgence. Blind Pharisee! First clean the inside of the cup and dish, and then the outside also will be clean.

What should a batterer believe about sex if he is to be truly repentant? The Bible and one's faith provide guidance. Abuse in any form, certainly including sexual abuse, is opposed to the basic principle of biblical teaching—unselfish love. 1 John 4:7–8 teaches, "Dear friends, let us love one another, for love comes from God. Everyone who loves has been born of God and knows God. Whoever does not love does not know God, because God is love."

A person who abuses another does not know love and does not know God. And Colossians 3:19 teaches, "Husbands, love your wives and do not be harsh with them," which clearly forbids physical or verbal spouse abuse. And then there is Mark 12:31, "Love your neighbor as yourself. There is no commandment greater than these."

Change Your Behavior

The New Testament's concept of love is agape: selfless, sacrificial, unconditional love that defines God's incomparable love for humankind. It is love without condition, and should govern your behavior toward others who need such love. In evaluating your relationship with an intimate partner, and whether your behavior conveys agape love, consider questions such as the following:

- Do you share power equally in your relationship?

- Do you respect the wishes of your partner regarding intimacy and physical or sexual contact?

- Can your partner trust that you will not betray or injure her, either intentionally or with acts that are reckless or intimidating?

- Are your partner's intimate interactions with you free and with full knowledge and consent?

- Do you wish the best for your partner?

- Do you accept responsibility for the consequences of your actions?

Hopefully you can answer yes to each of these questions. If you answer "no" to any of them, you can bet that you are not exhibiting agape love and your behavior is violating your relationship with your partner. If this is the case, repentance is in order. It should include adopting principles such as the following:

- Sexual activity should always be consensual, and your partner should have free choice in the matter.

- Sexual activity should take place in an environment of respect, caring, mutuality, and equality.

- Any form of force or abuse in the sexual experience is unacceptable.

As discussed in Chapter 4, repentance is not a one-time event, but is an ongoing, daily, hourly attitude and change of life. If you have engaged in sexual abuse and wish to repent, have these principles guide your attitude and behavior going forward.

Sexual Respect and Forgiveness

Chapter 12, Forgiving One Another, notes that forgiveness may involve you asking for forgiveness, being forgiven, and forgiving another. When you have sexually abused your partner, recognize that, even if you've committed to change, she most likely experienced a high degree of trauma and fear and may not feel safe around you, trust you—or be willing to forgive.

If your partner considers forgiveness, it can be at either of two levels. It may involve her telling you that she forgives you, giving you a pass, and moving on with life as a "clean slate." For example, Sue might forgive Carlos, while also refusing intimacy, moving out, and asking for a divorce. Or, her forgiveness might contemplate reconciliation and restoration of the relationship. Sue might forgive Carlos with a mutual expectation that they will stay together and engage in a "normal" sexual relationship in the future.

It's up to the victim to decide whether to forgive, and if so whether the forgiveness will involve full reconciliation and an attempt to restore the relationship. If a man insists on either, he is engaging in another form of abuse.

Stated again: if an abuser insists a victim forgive him and/or reconcile, he is trying another form of control and is continuing the abuse.

Review Chapter 11 and 12 to help you think about whether and how you should ask your partner for forgiveness. In this regard, two aspects of forgiveness, true in essentially all cases but especially pertinent in cases of sexual abuse, are important.

Don't Cry Wolf

Think about the old fable concerning a shepherd boy who repeatedly tells villagers that wolves are attacking his flock when they are not doing so. When one actually does, the boy again calls for help, but the villagers believe it is another false alarm so they don't respond and the sheep are eaten by the wolf.

Similarly, when you ask for forgiveness you should be remorseful, have repented and changed your ways, and not abuse her in the future. If you do not honor these conditions, you are "crying wolf," and there is no reason to expect your partner to believe you have changed. Don't ask for forgiveness unless you have truly repented and will not repeat the abuse in the future. Treat repentance and your accountability for your behavior as a lifelong commitment that requires making healthy, respectful choices every day in every circumstance, and not just something that occurs at the time you confess and seek forgiveness.

Accept That Your Partner May Refuse to Forgive You

Sometimes the hurt has been so bad, things have gone so far, that no amount of "I'm sorry" or "Please forgive me," even if sincere, will make any difference. Sexual abuse causes major physical and psychological hurts (outlined in more detail in Chapter 19) that engenders in the victim extreme trauma, usually continuing fear and often anger. The physical and psychological trauma from sexual abuse is so great that in such cases forgiving the perpetrator tends to inappropriately minimize the victim's suffering and may encourage him to continue to repeat the offense. This view holds that anger, hatred, and even vengeance are morally responsible, appropriate responses to serious sexual violations such as rape, particularly when the perpetrator is not repentant and continues to repeat the offense.

A person who has been seriously abused by an intimate partner may choose to withhold forgiveness as a way of preserving their self-worth and resisting or avoiding violent attacks in the future. This is particularly true if they believe the man is "crying wolf," and his desire for forgiveness is really just a backhanded request or demand for more sex and a continuing relationship. Reread the section on When There Is No Forgiveness in Chapter 12 for some ideas on dealing with this situation.

Sexual Respect and Reconciliation

Reconciliation, discussed in more detail in Chapter 14, is generally considered to be the coming together of two people, perhaps two who have been estranged, or who refuse to talk with one another, but it can also address all sorts of differences between people, within yourself, and between you and God. Here we will focus mainly on the question of whether consensual sexual activity is appropriate or possible in the future if you have sexually abused your partner.

Don't Try to Reconcile for the Wrong Reasons

After asking for forgiveness, and perhaps being told by a partner that she will forgive him, abusers frequently expect everything to go back to the way they were. Sometimes women may stay in abusive sexual relationships for a number of very complex and intertwined reasons. Sometimes they stay because of the tactics of the abuser, ranging from an insincere request for forgiveness, to bribery in the form of roses or a night out on the town, to further threats or actual physical violence: for example, threatening to challenge them for custody of children, get them fired, use mental health issues against them, cut them off financially, etc. Sometimes women feel they have no choice, and for good reasons. They may believe they need a man, even if he is abusive, to provide for their families, protect their children, or prevent homelessness. Sometimes they feel there is too much to lose—e.g., financial or support for children—if they draw the line and stop a sexual relationship. Sometimes women buy into the wrong religious beliefs held by their abuser, or rely on their hope that the batterer will change. All of these situations involve some level of pressure or coercion. If pressure and coercion are present, there is no real reconciliation.

Foster Real Reconciliation when Appropriate

An intimate partner who has been sexually abused may never be comfortable with the way things were, especially after a major incident or a long history of abusive behavior. Even if you, an abuser, claim to have changed and your partner has forgiven you, return to conditions of the past may not be feasible. She may forgive in her heart and still choose not to expose herself to your behavior any longer. It is quite natural that she will feel anxious that you will hurt her again, and her fear of being hurt again is valid and should be respected.

Reconciliation doesn't necessarily mean returning to the way things were. Instead, it can mean dealing with the consequences of past abuse, or simply agreeing on how to proceed in the future. For example, it could cover a range of situations, such as:

- Forgiveness and a peaceful, nonabusive divorce with no further contact.

- Forgiveness and a peaceful divorce with continuing peaceful contact that is beneficial to the children.

- An agreement to separate while the person who abused undertakes an appropriate intervention, such as a BIPP.

- An agreement to a relationship involving appropriate, consensual sex.

If you have not changed your life and abusive attitudes, a partner's refusal to return to the way things were is her only legitimate course of action. A form of reconciliation other than a return to the past, perhaps a peaceful divorce, might be the best alternative.

If you have taken responsibility for your actions, acknowledged that what you did was wrong, genuinely apologized, and changed your life, that is a good start toward reconciliation involving an appropriate relationship. However, depending upon the circumstances and your partner's feelings, this level of reconciliation could take a long time, or never happen. Only time, perhaps a very long time, will tell if you can live together in a committed relationship involving consensual sex.

In a reconciliation, remember that if you have sexually abused your partner, she has every right to dictate the terms of the future relationship she is willing to have with you, and to say, "This is what I'm comfortable with at this point, and no more, at least for now." Any attempted pressure or coercion by you would be just as unacceptable as your abuse in the first place. If some level of trust returns in the future, you can always deepen the intimacy of the relationship if your partner agrees.

Summary

A victim's forgiveness of and reconciliation with an abuser must be free and consensual, like sexual activity in the first place. If you insist on them, you are continuing the abuse. Your only appropriate alternative is to invite forgiveness and reconciliation by changing your behavior and living a repentant life.

Questions for Reflection or Group Study

1. What do Ephesians 5:33 and Matthew 23:25, quoted above, teach about sexual abuse and respect with an intimate partner?

2. Review the story of Carlos and Sue in the previous chapter. In the chart below, list four beliefs that you think Carlos held that contributed to his sexual abuse, and then list how each could be corrected to a belief that leads to sexual respect and mutuality.

Abusive Belief	Respectful Belief
1.	1.
2.	2.
3.	3.
4.	4.

SEXUAL RESPECT

3. What does this tell you about your own beliefs on the subject of sexual respect?

4. What does sexual respect mean to you?

5. Do you think Carlos should ask Sue for forgiveness relating to matters of sexual abuse? What does this teach about your situation?

6. If you have been involved in sexual abuse, should your partner forgive you? Why or why not?

7. Do you think Sue should be willing to reconcile with Carlos? Why or why not? How has Carlos' behavior made it so hard for Sue to forgive him?

8. What does it mean if you insist on either forgiveness or reconciliation?

Personal Reflection

Which of the learning objectives for this chapter is most important to you in stopping abuse and transforming your life? Why?

CHAPTER 21
Abusive Fatherhood

Learning Objectives

After completing this chapter, you should be able to:
- Accept that there is more to being a dad than just the biological contribution and the legal rights and obligations.
- Recognize and acknowledge the family, social, moral, and religious obligations of being a dad.
- Explain how a man's choice to abuse a partner ripples out to affect others in the family—particularly the children—and future generations.
- Describe how the same beliefs and desire for control that drive partner abuse often drive men to abuse children.
- Understand that children from abusive homes are typically in terrible pain and suffer many problems.

ALMOST ANY MAN CAN FATHER A CHILD. SOME people think of a father as just the male who provides the genes that result in a baby. Others think of fathers' obligations to provide financial support, care, and keeping for their children. But there is much more to being a dad than just providing the biological and financial contribution.

As an example, let's review the story of King David and his family from 2 Samuel 11–13 (introduced in Chapter 5, "Responsibility: Looking Back"). David, king of Israel, was in many ways an effective king, but he was a miserable failure as a father. He committed adultery with Bathsheba, and then arranged to have her husband, Uriah, killed. Amnon, David's firstborn son raped Tamar. Absalom, Tamar's brother and David's second son, had Amnon killed and then incited a rebellion against David. Adonijah, David's fourth son, took the throne that rightfully belonged to Solomon. Solomon, King David's seventh son, became King and was known for his wisdom. However, he had many wives and mistresses, worshipped false gods, and otherwise ignored God's teachings.

David's story is an example of one's own bad behavior affecting one's children and influencing who they become. This chapter explores how your behavior, like David's, can negatively affect your children and future generations. Chapter 22 offers suggestions for being a safe, effective father.

The Effect of Partner Abuse

The effects of partner abuse are broad and seemingly never-ending—often without boundaries or time limits. Chapter 5 introduced the ripple effect, suggesting that most abusive actions are like throwing a stone into a still, silent pond. The stone hits the water in one place, but its effects radiate out and down and affect the water in many places.

Similarly, abuse of a partner affects not only the partner, but also ripples broadly to others—particularly the children—and society in general. Partner abuse usually also ripples forward to affect people in the future—moving from grandparents to parents to children—as parents unknowingly teach their children to abuse others or to live with abuse from others.

The Ripple Effect on Children

If you choose to abuse your spouse, partner, or the mother of your children, you choose to abuse the children as well. It is next to impossible to keep such abuse from affecting them. Even if children are not a direct victim of physical violence, they are a victim of the abuse. They have a front-row seat, are watching, and are constantly learning from you. They are aware of the tension in the home arising from your abuse and their mother's fearfulness, and they often see actual incidents of physical and/or sexual abuse, hear threats or fighting noises from another room, or observe the aftermath of physical abuse such as blood, bruises, tears, torn clothing, and broken items.

One child described the situations as follows:

> We'd only hear, we wouldn't see her, we'd just hear her, and it would upset us. Sometimes it was actually quite annoying

hearing him as well, because mom was shouting back. We didn't mind hearing mom, but because we heard him shouting it made us angry . . . It made it hard to concentrate at school and all. I used to get 10 out of 10 in tests and then, when the fighting started, I only got like 8 out of 10, 7 out of 10. I couldn't concentrate as much. It would be all in my head and when I'd go to bed, I'd cry sometimes and I'd come down to mom.

Another child explained:

We'd wake up at night and Daddy would be yelling and shouting at Mommy after coming home drunk. My sisters would wake up, they'd sense something was going on, that there was something wrong with Mommy. They'd be saying, "Are you all right, Mommy?" And I'd be trying to shield them in another room and I'd have to look after them and say, you know, it's going to be all right, you know, that kind of a way. But it wouldn't be though.

A third child remembered:

I'd wake up in the middle of the night, and he'd be roaring and screaming. She'd be banging across the floor, you know what I mean, and I'd have to stay up listening to it and after a time I'd hear a thump, knowing well like that's Mommy downstairs, beaten up, and that's what hurt me. Sometimes, like, I felt like it was my fault, like why did I never stop it. Like why did I never go down and . . . It's horrible like. It's just, what if I went down . . . he would have stopped and, do you know, things like I remember the feeling and I still remember like I couldn't go downstairs. Like what if he did it to me or something. It was horrible . . .[15]

Children from abusive homes often look okay to the outside world, but they are typically in terrible pain and suffer various problems. These children often show elevated rates of psychological, emotional, and behavioral problems, including aggression and anxiety. They never know what will trigger the abuse, and therefore, never feel safe. They often become fearful and anxious, are continually on guard, watching and waiting for the next event to occur. They develop feelings of rage, embarrassment, and humiliation. They worry for themselves, their mother, and their siblings, and often feel worthless and powerless, isolated and vulnerable. They feel physically, emotionally and psychologically abandoned. They often experience sleep disturbances, sadness, depression, anger, stomachaches and/or headaches, bedwetting, and loss of ability to concentrate, resulting in poor school performance and attendance. They may experience developmental delays in speech, motor or mental skills. They may also use violence to express themselves, displaying increased aggression with peers or their mother. Children from violent homes have higher risks of alcohol/drug abuse, post-traumatic stress disorder, and juvenile delinquency. Witnessing domestic violence is the single situation that is most likely to lead to juvenile delinquency and adult criminality.

The Ripple Effect on Future Generations

The Ten Commandments, God's covenant with Israel, are a basis of the moral principles of the Western world. One of the commandments, Deuteronomy 5:7–10, states:

> You shall have no other gods before me. You shall not make for yourself an image in the form of anything in heaven above or on the earth beneath or in the waters below. You shall not bow down to them or worship them; for I, the Lord your God, am a jealous God, punishing the children for the sin of the parents to the third and fourth generation of those who hate me, but showing love to a thousand generations of those who love me and keep my commandments.

Although there are differing opinions as to the precise meaning of these words, we understand them to suggest that children are likely to imitate their abusive fathers, (as they would idolaters) and when they do, God will be "punishing the children for the sin of the parents to the third and fourth generation of those who hate me, . . ." We take it to be another biblical example of the ripple effect of spousal abuse that includes future generations of parents and children.

Importantly, an abusive dad affects all of the children's relationships, including those with friends, lovers, and spouses—currently and in the future. Children who grow up witnessing their father using abuse for power and control while stripping away their mother's autonomy and rights, grow up with a role model of intimate relationships in which one person uses intimidation and violence over the other person, and in one way or another the other person lives with it.

Some girls who grow up in an abusive environment often think that's how Daddy shows love to Mom, and when they grow up and find someone in the same situation, they think it is normal and don't see anything wrong with it.

Adolescent boys may identify with an abusive father or father figure who tells them their mother provoked or deserved the violence, which influences them to display aggression in their own relationships and blame others.

Such behavior, by both girls and boys, is almost certain to be repeated again and again, and become part of a cycle of violence that is generational. Once started, it may be handed down from generation to generation, like an unfortunate family tradition. Children raised in a chaotic, abusive environment are much more likely to grow up and repeat the same behavior when they are adults.

These cycles of violence are tragic for the children who experience them. Only the person who is the batterer can break the cycle and prevent abuse of his grandchildren, and he can begin to do that by stopping the battering now, owning up to his past use of violence, and repairing the relationship with his children.

Child Abuse

We saw in Chapter 4 that men's desire for control drives most partner abuse. This perceived need is often fostered by a number of other associated beliefs, such as a feeling of entitlement, selfishness and self-centeredness, a superiority complex, disrespect of others, possessiveness, and confusing love and abuse.

Unfortunately, the same beliefs and desire for control frequently cause men to treat children in much the same way they deal with their partner. One child described her father's abuse as follows:

> My father thought that it was necessary for children to fear their parents in order to behave. He thought that kids were born bad. He was physically abused as a child by his own father, and then fought in Vietnam, so my father told himself that as long as he didn't beat us with his fists, that he was doing a good job

as a father, and that every other cruelty was a necessary childrearing tool. My mother never interfered with his cruelty. He belittled and humiliated her every chance he got. He needed to feel smarter and bigger than everyone else.

My father was always angry and always ready to explode at any time. His life was hard, and he thought it was crucial for me and my four siblings to understand this from the age of two years old on. Just his voice, or the sound of his car pulling up to the house, was enough to make my stomach flip, my body to flush with heat and sweat, my face to tingle, my mind to fill with panic and dread. Every single day. I would go completely still, feeling that if I became wallpaper, he wouldn't see me. The worst thing imaginable was being noticed, because no good ever came of it.[16]

Bad parenting and child abuse can range from indifference and ignoring the child's needs for emotional support, up to and including violence. Discussed below are three forms. All are abusive to children and their mothers, and all cause trauma and have lasting impacts. All teach children negative models of relationships which often contribute to generational abuse.

Passive, Distant, Indifferent Fathers

Children have both physical and emotional needs. The abusive beliefs and attitudes of many men, involving feelings of entitlement, selfishness, and self-centeredness developed through generations of unhealthy behavior, cause the men to fail to meet these needs and act as though fatherhood is not an important responsibility. This is particularly true of those who have walked out on their families, are frequently unemployed, are affected by substance use, or are incarcerated from time to time. Whatever the circumstance, such individuals often show a lack of responsibility toward their children and lay their parenting obligations on someone else.

Other men, including those who live in the same home with children, seem to assume that the father's only role in the family is to be the breadwinner and look out for himself. Work or other interests are more important than being present as a father. They typically spend little time at home, pass parenting responsibility to their spouse, and do not take a significant role in being a father for their children.

Even when a father is physically present and takes care of all the necessities of life, he may be emotionally unavailable, some would even say passive abusive. Mostly he just doesn't seem to care, doesn't teach or mentor his children or even listen when they talk to him, and doesn't know much about them. His relationship is dismissive and disinterested. He focuses on other interests or being at work, and limits his parenting to concrete tasks ("men's work"), like pumping up a bike tire, while the children use their mother for emotional support. He considers his own needs and independence as a man—male entitlement—as more important than his duties as a father.

Authoritarian Fathers

Abusive attitudes such as desire for control, possessiveness, a superiority complex, or disrespect of others tend to drive abusive men toward authoritarian parenting that not only affects the children but also inhibits their mother's ability to safely parent them. They become restrictive, punishment-heavy parents who don't encourage verbal give-and-take; expect orders to be obeyed without question; and tend to control children through shaming, the withdrawal of love, or other forms of punishment. They often don't attempt to explain the reasons for rules. Extreme value is placed on obedience with an indisputable deference to authority. Yelling and spanking of younger children is used to control their behavior. Generally, authoritarian parents are not very emotional or affectionate and are often critical of their children if they fail to meet their expectations.

Kids with authoritarian parents may be relatively well-behaved, because they are afraid to be otherwise. But they also tend to be less resourceful, have poorer social skills and lower self-esteem, and achieve less at school than children with more positive parents. They feel pressure to conform, rarely learn to think on their own, may become angry, resentful, and frustrated, and resent authority.

Abusive Fathers

Passive, indifferent, and authoritarian fathers are abusive and neglectful if they use such behaviors to control their family and the level of responsibility they afford them. Fathers who abuse their children are, much like most abusers, hostile, demanding, and entitled men who generally are controlling toward both their partners and their children. They typically have rigid and unreasonable rules and little patience. They expect to be obeyed unquestionably, do not take criticism, advice, or any resistance from their family, and use strict and abusive means to ensure their children do what they are told to do.

Violent fathers focus more on control and punishment than on the teaching aspects of discipline. They try to justify their use of control by claiming a desire to protect their children from outside harm or to prevent them from developing bad behaviors.

Child abuse and neglect has been defined as any recent act or failure to act on the part of a parent or caregiver that results in death, serious physical or emotional harm, sexual abuse or exploitation, or any act or failure to act that presents an imminent risk of serious harm. Child abuse may come in many forms, including emotional/psychological, physical, and sexual. Emotional and psychological abuse typically includes verbal or emotional debasement of a child. Physical abuse may include assault, attack, and harming of a child through the use of force, violence, or any other of a variety of physical means intended for bodily harm. Sexual abuse involves any abuse that is sexual in nature or involves a sexual act against a child.

The effects of abuse on children go beyond the physical harm that often is imposed. They include anxiety, depression, difficulty concentrating, academic problems in school-age children and adolescents, withdrawal and/or difficulty connecting with others, flashbacks, and difficulty sleeping. Abuse may result in lowered expectations of self and poor treatment by others. This can make the survivor of childhood abuse a risk for becoming a victim in adulthood.

Summary

A father has a broad parenting role that goes well beyond financial support. Partner abuse nearly always has a ripple effect that negatively affects children in the family and future generations. Unfortunately, the characteristics that cause a man to abuse a spouse or partner frequently prevent him from being an effective parent and may lead to unhealthy parenting choices that are child abuse and neglect.

All abuse must be stopped. Chapter 22 discusses a better way of parenting that is not abusive.

Questions for Reflection or Group Study

1. List three things you learned from Deuteronomy 5:7–10.

2. How would you describe yourself as a father—and how has your abuse of a partner affected your parenting?

3. Demonstrate the ripple effect of partner abuse by describing an example of an abusive situation (that occurred in your family if applicable) and then listing the direct victim(s) and other child victims, and how the children were affected.

    Abusive situation:

ABUSIVE FATHERHOOD

Direct victim(s):

First indirect victim(s):

Second indirect victim(s):

Other indirect victim(s):

4. The narrative describes three types of fathers: those who are passive, distant, or indifferent; those who are authoritarian; and those who are abusive. Does any category describe your father? Explain.

5. What were the consequences for your children of your father's parenting of you?

6. List three mistakes you believe you have made in parenting children—or if you are not a parent, define three poor choices that impacted your being a positive role model to youth in your family.

ABUSIVE FATHERHOOD

7. Describe the role model you need to provide for your children or others under your influence.

> **Personal Reflection**
>
> Which of the learning objectives for this chapter is most important to you in stopping abuse and transforming your life? Why?

CHAPTER 22
Positive Parenting

Learning Objectives

After completing this chapter, you should be able to:
- Stop abusing your partner and support her as a mother.
- Become a positive role model for your child.
- Become a servant-leader for your family.
- Better allocate the time you spend with your children.
- Use positive discipline rather than punishment when correction is necessary.

IF YOU ARE A FATHER (OR ARE IN A POSITION to interact with or influence a child) who has abused your partner, you may think the children have not been pulled into or affected by abuse in your home, and that you have met all your parenting obligations. But not likely! As discussed in Chapter 21, many abusers fulfill their financial and legal obligations to their children, but fail miserably in becoming a positive parent.

The key to becoming a positive parent is summarized in an article published in the August 1999 *Readers Digest* citing Mother Teresa. Mother Teresa had given a speech about her work with the sick and dying and orphans in India. A member of the audience asked, "You have done so much to make the world a better place. What can we do?" Mother Teresa smiled and simply said, "Love your children. There are other things you can do, but that is the best. Love your children. Love your children as much as you can. That is the best."[17]

And think about the words of Deuteronomy 6:5–9, sometimes called the "*Magna Carta* of the home."

> Love the Lord your God with all your heart and with all your soul and with all your strength. These commandments that I give you today are to be on your hearts. Impress them on your children. Talk about them when you sit at home and when you

walk along the road, when you lie down and when you get up. Tie them as symbols on your hands and bind them on your foreheads. Write them on the doorframes of your houses and on your gates.

Similarly, Proverbs 22:6 teaches, "Start children off on the way they should go, and even when they are old they will not turn from it."

These Scripture tell us to live in ways that pass God's truths to future generations. Doing so means if you are a dad you need to meet your many family, social, moral, and religious obligations. In this chapter, we will not try to cover all these issues or fully address the broad and complex subject of parenting. Instead, the following sections suggest five simple principles, closely related and overlapping, that can help you stop your abuse and be a positive father.

Support Your Partner

The role of both father and mother is important in effective parenting. Each needs to be a teacher, nurturer, and anchor of the children, as well as an educator, disciplinarian, and confidant that provides the emotional backbone for the children and family.

Being an effective parent is a very difficult job, even with the help of a loving partner. If you abuse and try to control your children's mother—use physical violence against her, assault the child, or emotionally or physically injure either of them—you make it almost impossible for her to be an effective parent. Whether you are the biological father, stepfather, or the mother's boyfriend, your controlling or abusive behavior poses a risk to the well-being of the children in your life, and may even cause a child to hurt his or her mother. Your abuse makes the job of mothering so much harder. Your abuse may cause parenting problems for your partner in many ways. For example, it may:

- Drive a wedge between the mother and her children—perhaps by obligating her to work extra hours or persuading her that her attachment to her children is unhealthy or unnatural.

- Make her choose between siding with her child and you, or between spending time with her child and spending time with you.

- Undermine her by finding ways to become the only authority in the house and by encouraging children to disrespect their mother.

- Obligate her to use harsher discipline than she thinks she should.

- Bribe, push, or inspire children into degrading or spying on their mother or even hurting her physically.

The consequences of undermining your spouse's parenting are significant, and bad. Your children miss out on bonding with both parents, and may see one or the other as deeply flawed instead of seeing both parents as equals who are devoted to caring for and nurturing them. Children may, in essence, see you as pitting them against your partner and respond by manipulating each of you to get what they want. They may begin to view you as "good cop" and your spouse as "bad cop," further enabling them to manipulate as much as they want to. This all is likely to lead to more controlling behavior in the relationship; and bitterness and difficulty in your marriage.

Parenting should be a team effort, involving both father and mother. Biblical teaching clearly supports the idea of children listening to and honoring both parents—strongly implying that fathers should support and work with their children's mother in ways that lead the children to honor and respect both of them. For example, Exodus 20:12 states, "Honor your father and your mother, so that you may live long in the land the Lord your God is giving you." Proverbs 1:8 reads, "Listen, my son, to your father's instruction and do not forsake your mother's teaching. Ephesians 6:12 states, "Children, obey your parents in the Lord, for this is right. Honor your father and mother."

Each parent plays important and different roles, and usually have different styles, in promoting their children's well-being, by supporting their physical, intellectual, emotional, and social development. As a father, you need to fulfil your own role and also support your partner. To support her, you can:

- Seriously consider the impact of your past violence on your parenting—how it has created barriers to communication and negotiations and how you can change the situation.

- Accept that you are on the same team, and not fighting against each other. You are supposed to be working together to raise your children with love.

- Get together on your key values. When both parents teach and reinforce the same values, different parenting styles are rarely a problem.

- Support sensitive, responsive relationships between your partner and the children.

- Help your partner feel good about herself in her role as a parent. She can then safely parent and transfer this feeling of approval to the children.

- Support your partner's decisions and actions. Children learn quickly how to pit one parent against the other and drive a wedge between Mom and Dad. Try not to disagree on parenting in front of the kids. If one of you has to let the other parent take the lead in a given situation, let that happen and then talk about it later.

- Find the appropriate balance between parenting beliefs and styles by negotiating your differences. Lots of communicating, talking about your differences, and then cooperating and compromising will help.

- Get help if it is not working. If you find yourself in regular conflict over parenting decisions after your abuse has stopped, you might consider talking together with a family therapist, a clergy member, or a trusted friend who seems to be a successful parent, or attending a parenting class.

Working together to peacefully and effectively parent your children takes a lot of work and attention. But the positive impact on your children of your support of your wife, and the two of you working together, will be worth all the work.

Be a Positive Role Model

Think about it. If you abuse your child's mother, you abuse your child, and probably your grandchildren as well! You may not hit your children, or directly intimidate them—but you evade your responsibility, interrupt their mother's ability to parent, and hurt them just the same. You become a role model that teaches them to behave badly, which creates the likelihood that they will carry the hurt to future generations.

You can run but you can't hide! You are a role model for your child, for better or worse. Your children will see your example—positive or negative—as a pattern for the way life is to be lived. The emotional environment you establish in the home, the child-rearing style you use, and the kind of behavior you model, all have a major influence on your child's development. Instead of having your children observe your abuse, let them catch you being good.

Instead of being a model of abusive behavior, you can become a model of a healthy partner and father—whether you are a biological father, living with your child or living elsewhere, divorced from your child's mother, a step-father, gay or straight, working or stay-at-home. Role modeling is one of the most powerful tools you have in your parenting tool belt to influence the direction of your children's character and behavior. You can model the values you want your children to adopt so they become the adults you would like them to be.

Being a positive role model requires effort, forethought, and self-control. You need to be very intentional about the behavior you model for your children. The following thoughts should help:

- Teach through your own actions: Consider what kind of people you want your children to become, and then act as they would act. This includes all your behavior, but particularly not abusing your partner and instead treating her with dignity and respect.

- Walk the talk: Children can see hypocrisy immediately, and seeing it in you sends them looking for alternative role models. Therefore, live by the rules you preach.

- Watch your words: Your children are not only watching you carefully for clues about how to be; they are also listening to you. The way you speak, what you speak about, and the opinions you express will influence their values and behavior.

- Build strong relationships: You will be a larger influence in your children's lives if you have a good relationship with them. Give them unconditional love in a safe environment that provides consistent, firm, and flexible discipline, as discussed below.

- Forgive mistakes: Nobody is perfect—neither you nor your children. That means that mistakes will be made. Forgive them for theirs. Take responsibility and be accountable for yours.

The essence of being a role model is perhaps best summarized in the words of Saint Francis of Assisi, one of the most venerated religious figures in Roman Catholic history: "Do all you can to preach the gospel and if necessary use words!"

Be a Servant-Leader

The term "family" means different things under different circumstances. For our purpose, a family is a collective unit of human beings comprised of you, your partner and/or your children's mother, and the children to whom you have parental obligations, all of whom have an emotional connection with each other. Families have a feel, an aura, a style, a life of their own. They are sad or happy; they demonstrate love, pain, or ambivalence; they are dysfunctional or effective.

Fostering a happy, loving, effective family is perhaps your greatest responsibility as a father and parent. This cannot be accomplished with demands for control, possessiveness, a feeling of entitlement and emphasis on self, or other attitudes so often exhibited by those who abuse. Instead, building a positive family is a journey that will require patience, persistence, and thoughtful attention. You can have the status, power, and resources to complete the journey by becoming a servant-leader.

The term servant-leader is of fairly modern vintage, but the concept is old, captured in Mark 10:42–45:

> Jesus called them together and said, "You know that those who are regarded as rulers of the Gentiles lord it over them, and their high officials exercise authority over them. Not so with you. Instead, whoever wants to become great among you must be your servant, and whoever wants to be first must be slave of all. For even the Son of Man did not come to be served, but to serve, and to give his life as a ransom for many."

Servant-leaders are both servants and leaders. Traditional leaders generally see themselves at the "top of the pyramid," and use their position there to exercise power and control. Servant-leaders are different.

Servant-leaders share power and make sure other family members' needs and wants are honored first, causing them to grow and become happier, healthier, wiser, freer, and more fulfilled. Adhering to simple principles such as the following will be help you become a servant-leader.

- Demonstrate moral integrity: It is impossible to serve and lead others without their trust, loyalty, and respect. To gain them from others, you must exhibit moral integrity in all you do. And this starts with honesty. Honesty can be demonstrated in many ways. Admitting personal weaknesses is among the best. Admitting your weakness not only encourages the respect of family members, but also helps to establish an environment of trust, which goes a long way toward making other things doable.

- Respect family members: There are many ways to show respect for family members. First, treat them as individuals, and attempt to understand their values, aspirations, and beliefs. Let them know that they have priority over people and concerns from outside the family. Be an encourager. Affirm their value, and express sincere appreciation for them as valuable human beings.

- Go beyond your self-interest: Servant-leaders need to do things of lasting importance that family members will recognize as beneficial to them. To be a servant-leader, you must be willing to put your "skin in the game," and show family members how they will benefit from your actions at least as much as, and ideally more than, you do.

- Listen: Communication and decision-making skills are important for the servant-leader, and they need to be reinforced by a deep commitment to listening intently to family members. Chapter 18 addresses these issues in some detail. The important thing is to identify and clarify the will of family members so you can respond appropriately. You also need to listen to your own inner voice. Listening, coupled with periods of reflection, is essential to your growth as an effective servant-leader.

- Empathize: The servant-leader strives to understand and empathize with others. Empathy, walking a mile in the other's sandals, as discussed in more detail in Chapter 6, allows you to see things from family members' points of view and make connections. Seeing things from their perspective helps you recognize and accept their special and unique spirits, assume their good intentions, and not reject them as people, even when you refuse to accept certain of their behavior.

- Exhibit unconditional love: Sometimes all of us feel like we are unlovable, but in strong families each member knows that no matter how unlovable they might act, their family members will always love them. A servant-leader consistently demonstrates the unconditional love that strengthens the bonds that tie the family together.

Spend Time with Your Children

Fathers often claim great difficulty in spending much time with their children. Many responsibilities and stressors can get in the way of doing so. You may have a demanding job, or have a lot of responsibilities that limit your time. Or your use of violence in the past may have resulted in court orders that limit your time with your children. Your partner may not believe it is safe for the children to spend time with you unsupervised because of your use of violence or past reckless or threatening behavior. However, despite these constraints, you have a responsibility, to the extent feasible, to be an active, engaged supportive parent to your children and a witness to their lives. When you care enough to spend time with your children you show them in concrete terms that they are important, and you build their self-esteem, which makes it easier for them to build relationships. Your gift of your time also helps children develop stronger relationships, makes handling stressful situations easier, teaches them important life lessons, and can create wonderful memories.

Spending time with your children means creating good times, but more importantly, it also means being there when things are tough, and being an active participant in your child's everyday struggles. This of course, requires time, patience, and a willingness to participate in a long-term process. You can find time for your children if you make them your priority. You can weed out the activities that take up too much time and create parenting plans that serve the interests of your children. This means saying "no" more often to people and activities that aren't central to your lives. As always, it's a balancing act. Some tips for expanding and benefiting from your time with your child, if allowed, include:

- Have a daily time to connect. If being together is not possible, create a routine such as leaving a note or making a scheduled phone call.

- Create a special ritual or activity that can be done about the same time every day.

- Tell your children you love them every day.

- Reinforce positive behavior by acknowledging it and expressing your appreciation.

- Have meals together whenever possible.

- Do activities of your children's choosing together.

- Play with your children.

- Turn off technology when you are spending time with your children.

Emphasize the quality of the time you spend with your children. Your time together allows you to become a good role model and a servant-leader who provides the support and reassurance your child needs.

Use Positive Discipline

It's safe to assume that your children sometimes will act out, engage in conflict with you, or otherwise not meet your expectations. You may need to impose discipline to help them change the offending behavior and behave better in the future.

"Discipline" and "punishment" sometimes are used interchangeably, but "positive discipline" and "punishment" are two very different approaches to dealing with your child's behavior, as seen in the chart on the next page.

Punishment involves imposing a penalty on your children as a matter of retribution or getting even. It looks backward and seeks to have your children suffer some type of pain for their past misbehavior. Punishment reduces communication and drives your children's bad behavior underground because they are afraid of what will happen if you become aware of it. It does nothing to help your children do what they cannot already do or learn from their mistakes.

Punishment	Positive Discipline
Inflicts Pain	Instructs
Uses force, violence, and intimidation	Uses respect and firm limits
Instills fear	Instills love
Instills guilt	Instills accountability
Judges	Accepts
Manipulates	Teaches
Blames	Empathizes
Forces	Expects
Uses retribution	Uses consequences

Fear is the main reason punishment causes compliance, and children often lose their fear after continual exposure to the same punishment. Therefore, punishment loses its effectiveness over time, as your children become insensitive to it and its sanctions. Your children will develop apathy, anger, resentment, and frustration over the longer term. They may feel guilty, but this does nothing to improve behavior. They may behave as you wish, but only to avoid punishment and not because they have learned or believe it is the right thing to do.

Positive discipline looks to the future to help your children learn, grow, and develop values and a conscience that respects the rights of others and the difference between right and wrong. It does not disregard the past, but uses it as a platform for learning and development. Positive discipline is the intervention that is most likely to lead to good behavior and minimize conflict over time.

Positive discipline may include a form of punishment or penalty, but it is only a means to the end. Punishment in connection with positive discipline is an action that helps you express your love and respect, teach your children, and get healthy, happy children currently and in the future. The principles introduced in the following sections should help you use positive discipline.

Discipline Yourself

Act like you want your children to act—and first and foremost avoid any abuse of your partner, the children's mother, or the children. Maintain the same basic ethical and moral standards, the same characteristics of responsibility, and the same honor and respect for others as you expect from your children. Do anything less, and your children will see the hypocrisy of your actions, and your attempts to discipline them will fail.

For more detail on disciplining yourself, review the previous sections on being a positive role model, providing servant-leadership, and spending time with your child.

Set Clear, Affirmative Expectations

Your children cannot comply if they don't know what to comply with. Disciplining them when they don't clearly understand why will make you appear to be a monster, out to punish rather than teach. On the other hand, clear and unequivocal expectations are the ultimate leverage. If your children know they must, they probably will! They will comply, not because they are afraid, but because they know there is no alternative.

For more detail on setting clear, affirmative expectations, see Chapter 18, Peaceful Communication.

Use Consequences to Enforce and Teach

Seeing the consequences—the results—of their actions is your children's best teacher. Legitimate, fair consequences teach children that actions cause reactions, causes have effects, behavior leads to results, and they can control those responses by how they act and behave. Consequences teach responsibility when children face the predictable results of their actions and learn to adopt those choices that have the best consequences. Natural consequences involve letting your children make mistakes and then deal with the reasonable, logical ramifications of their poor choices. For example, they leave toys outside, you don't intervene, and rain ruins them. A challenge in dealing with the natural consequence of your children's misbehavior is to: (1) not inappropriately bail them out and instead allow them to learn from their mistakes by suffering the consequences, and (2) protect them from truly bad consequences. This requires you to thoughtfully and with love allow them to deal with their own problems, to the extent they are able, as a way of teaching them to avoid problems in the future.

Sometimes you cannot allow natural consequences to occur—like when you child starts to run across a busy street. In such cases, you may need to impose consequences in the form of appropriate penalties that are related to their action. For example, if a child runs into a street, you might abruptly stop them, explain why their act was scary for you, why it was dangerous, and how you're going to hold hands in future outings when near a street. Imposed penalties can be an effective parenting tool, but they can backfire over the long run if the consequences become punishment rather than discipline. Thus your real challenge is to impose consequences that are reasonably related to their actions, and from which your children learn, rather than punishment that just makes them suffer. Review the section on Positive Discipline and follow the principles outlined there to ensure that the consequences you impose benefit your child and do not abuse him or her.

Questions for Reflection or Group Study

1. In the left column of the chart below list five desirable characteristics you believe your children would like in their father. In the column on the right, describe what you would need to do to demonstrate those characteristics.

Desirable Characteristics my Children Would Like	How I Can Demonstrate Such Characteristics
1.	1.
2.	2.
3.	3.
4.	4.
5.	5.

2. What does your response to question 1 say about you as a role model?

3. Describe in your own words what it means to be your family's servant-leader.

4. Considering your current situation, how much time do you believe you should spend in personal contact with your child each week? Explain. How will you support their mother in the process?

5. Circle the three characteristics from the lists below that best describe how you believe you should respond to children who misbehave or don't meet your expectations. Underline the three that you believe are least appropriate.

Positive Discipline
Instruct
Use respect and firm limits
Instill love
Instill accountability
Accept
Teach
Empathize
Expect
Use consequences

Punishment
Inflict pain
Use force/violence/intimidation
Instill fear
Instill guilt
Judge
Manipulate
Blame
Force
Use retribution

6. List three things you should do to better discipline yourself and explain why.

7. What do your responses to the questions above tell you about being a father?

Personal Reflection

Which of the learning objectives for this chapter is most important to you in stopping abuse and transforming your life? Why?

CHAPTER 23

Trust

> ### Learning Objectives
>
> After completing this chapter, you should be able to:
> - Build trust in your relationship with your partner, so that she can rely on your character, ability, strength, and truth.
> - Understand that insisting that your partner be trustworthy is in fact a technique of control used to abuse her.
> - Recognize the ways you can destroy a trusting relationship with your partner.
> - Take appropriate actions to change yourself and rebuild broken trust.
> - Accept the Golden Rule of Matthew 7:12 as a great summary of how to maintain trust: "So in everything, do to others what you would have them do to you, for this sums up the Law and the Prophets."

TONYA AND SAM HAD EACH RECENTLY ENDED separate romantic relationships, and were interested in getting back into the dating scene, though with no current serious intentions. They signed up with a popular online dating site, were matched, and soon began exchanging emails, at least one a day for a few weeks. They agreed to a date after about six weeks of emails and hour-long phone calls, and met in a local bookstore. Both were pleased, and perhaps a little surprised, that their pictures were pretty accurate and up to date—and they liked what they saw. They dated slowly in the beginning, spending time on long walks, over drinks, or just hanging out really getting to know one another, talking about everything from religion to children to death, where they seemed to have very similar beliefs. They never stood each other up or let each other down. They came to know each other pretty well, and both felt their relationship was like a dream come true. They soon became intimate, then began talking marriage. They married eighteen months after that first email.

Almost without realizing it, during their courtship and early marriage, Sam and Tonya had built what appeared to be a trusting relationship. They seemed they were honest with one another, said what they meant, and did what they said they would do. They communicated well and made mostly joint decisions. They weren't overly emotional, but honestly shared their feelings. Each tried to do what they thought was right, look out for the other, and admit their mistakes when they made them. They demonstrated trust and never belittled or looked with condescension at the other.

Trust

Trust is the confident belief that someone will behave in certain ways, based on commonly shared understandings or norms in a relationship or among members of the community: the firm belief in the reliability, truth, ability, or strength of someone or something. If I trust you, I can rely on you to make every effort to behave consistent with accepted norms and do what you say you will do. When I trust you, I have a feeling of comfort and safety with you. A borrowed short story illustrates the meaning of trust:

> A little girl and her father were crossing a bridge. The father was kind of scared so he asked his little daughter, "Sweetheart, please hold my hand so that you don't fall into the river."
>
> The little girl said, "No, Dad. You hold my hand."
>
> "What's the difference?" asked the puzzled father.
>
> "There's a big difference,"' replied the little girl. "If I hold your hand and something happens to me, chances are that I may let your hand go. But if you hold my hand, I know for sure that no matter what happens, you will never let my hand go." [18]

In any relationship, the essence of trust is confidence in one another. We need to hold the hand of the person who loves us rather than expecting them to hold ours.

Mutual trust is important in every aspect of any successful relationship—finances, intimacy, communication, spirituality, dealing with children, etc. If you trust your partner you can depend on her to act with integrity, ability, or character, according to shared understandings or community norms. If your partner trusts you, she can depend on you and know that you will act with integrity, ability, or character, according to shared understandings or community norms—which means, among other things, she will know that you will not abuse her.

Mutual trust allows you to honestly and faithfully deal with your partner and with whatever issues arise, and develop a relationship where each person's needs are met. People who trust another treat them with respect, and defer to their desires. You show your trust by treating your partner with honesty and dignity, respecting her boundaries, never abusing her, and being accountable to her.

Unfortunately, sometimes showing trust toward another is motivated by fear and a perceived need for obedience. In this situation, a person defers to status, authority, or power because they are afraid of the consequences if they don't. For example, a wife is home when her spouse wants her to be because she is afraid of what he will do if she isn't. Or a child obeys his mother's boyfriend out of fear of what he will do rather than actual trust.

Do others defer to you and do what you want? If so, is this show of deference because they trust you, or because you are bigger, meaner, can hurt them if they don't defer to you, and they fear you?

Fear is poisonous and tears us down, while trust builds us up. Fear is life-threatening, but trust makes life better. Fear is forced, trust is earned. Importantly, trust cannot be demanded or forced, though sometimes people mistakenly believe that it can. Trust is earned.

Mutual trust is built with honesty, communication, respect, and other behavior that help those involved know what to expect and live in security, without fear.

Breaking Trust

A cycle develops in many relationships: trust is established, trust is broken, and (hopefully) trust is re-established. When trust is broken, people don't know what to expect, and insecurity, isolation, and fear can lead to pain, misunderstandings, arguments, and stress. You can break your partner's trust in two ways.

When you, for whatever reason, fail to deliver on your promises or your partner's appropriate and reasonable expectations, or act inconsistently with your or her values or abuse her, you are not trustworthy, violate your partner's trust, and cause distrust between the two of you. For example, you break the trust relationship if you fail to make an effort to support your family, are not honest with your partner, or cheat on her.

Second, you can use the issue of trust to try to control—and therefore abuse—your partner. In the case of Sam and Tonya, splinters began to appear in their mutual trust, and the trust seemed to be breaking, when Sam claimed he just didn't have a feeling of trust, began to accuse her of violating his trust, and started insisting she behave differently.

Over time, Sam behaved as follows—while blaming his controlling behavior on "lack of trust."

- No matter what Tonja said or how she acted, Sam didn't believe her or feel like he could depend on her.

- He constantly accused her, judged her, or put words into her mouth over the most ridiculous things.

- He got overly jealous, negative, and defensive, which tended to push her further away.

- Sam became jealous of her relationship with other people and tended to try to keep her away from them, viewing conversations with anyone other than himself as a threat.

- He made her feel bad, constantly criticizing her and pointing out her mistakes and what she had done wrong in their relationship.

As time passed, Sam's desire to control everything became more obvious, and he kept Tonja in constant fear. He would push her, throw things at her, call her names, humiliate her in front of friends. These episodes were often followed by him apologizing but then harassing her to make up and show her trust by having sex with him.

Sam told himself, and a couple of friends, that he didn't trust Tonya. The truth is he was trying to control her and using a lack of trust to justify his controlling and abusive behavior. Similarly, when you insist your partner be trustworthy, you probably are using a form of control where you equate your trust with her compliance with your wants.

Lack of trust, like anger and substance abuse, does not cause domestic abuse, which is a choice abusive men make. However, lack of trust—really desire for control—can trigger distorted thinking that leads to abusive events, makes them worse, and makes the abuse more difficult for the victim to deal with.

Rebuilding Trust

Sometimes your partner will not behave in a trustworthy manner. This may involve an actual breach of trust, or it may be just your claim that you couldn't trust your partner because you didn't get what you wanted. No matter what has happened, further abuse through attempts to further control or to change your partner is not an acceptable option. To try to rebuild trust, you need to control and change yourself. Ask yourself how you have behaved abusively and justified it by claiming a lack of trust. How can you act responsibly and be accountable in the future to demonstrate you are trustworthy?

You can't change the past or completely avoid the baggage of your life. And you can't force someone to trust you, nor can another person force you to trust her. The issue is "feeling," not action. But trust can be earned.

You earn another's trust by doing things that show you can be trusted. It's like a boomerang: what you send out will come back to you. If you trust others, they are more likely to trust you.

You cannot control your partner. You can only control yourself, and behave with regular, honest, and cooperative behavior. On a practical level, this includes giving worth and value to your partner's feelings, needs, thoughts, ideas, wishes, and preferences by accepting her as an individual, unique person of value. It recognizes the good and the honorable in her.

To earn another's trust, treat them with dignity, kindness, and courtesy, giving basic consideration to their feelings. If you hurt another person, either verbally or physically, or reject him or her, you create fear, which undermines trust. Similarly, trying to control others undermines their sense of security and will push them away and make it more difficult for them to trust you. Trust builds an atmosphere of security and safety. Treating your partner with dignity involves empathy, or seeing the world as she sees it, walking in her shoes. When you empathize with her, and put yourself in her shoes, you are likely to treat her with dignity, and it will be possible for you to build the emotional connections that lead to increased trust in the relationship.

To restore trust, you have to look at yourself and almost certainly change yourself. Characteristics and actions such as those discussed in the following paragraphs will help.

Be Honest in All You Say and Do

Sooner or later most things come to light, and the consequences of not being truthful will kill trust and ruin your relationship. To build trust, tell the truth, mean what you say, and don't sugarcoat the truth. Be honest with yourself and with your victim about the violence and abuse you have used in the past. Don't keep things hidden unless you believe revealing them will unnecessarily hurt the other person. When another person knows they can depend on the truthfulness of whatever comes out of your mouth, then you are building trust.

Always be Reliable

Trust means people can rely on you: your partner, child, or other person you are dealing with can predict what you will do and count on you to do the right thing. Being reliable also means you are faithful on all levels—physically but also emotionally. You do what you have said you will do, whether in marriage vows or in other ways, verbal or nonverbal. You are committed to nonviolence and non-controlling behavior. People trust you because you deliver on their expectations.

Respect Yourself

Self-respect is often defined as a sense of worth or as due respect for oneself. It often includes self-esteem, self-confidence, dignity, self-love, a sense of honor, self-reliance, and pride. It is the opposite of shame, putting one's self down, arrogance, and self-importance. Self-respect includes being strong enough to admit when you're wrong and apologize without feeling threatened, and the confidence to allow people to be themselves without being controlled by you.

If you have low self-respect, your confidence in self and in others is also low, making it difficult to trust others because of your difficulty in handling the consequences if they don't deliver on your expectations. On the other hand, higher self-respect means you can trust others because you are willing and able to handle the consequences if they should break your trust. In summary, having the self-respect to trust yourself helps you trust others.

Respect Boundaries

Personal boundaries are typically unstated guidelines or rules that people set to place limits on how other people behave toward them. They may include physical, mental, psychological, and spiritual boundaries. For example, your partner might set personal boundaries that, "I'm not willing to talk to you unless your voice is calm," or "sex is out of the question for now." You may set boundaries by sometimes honestly and reliably saying no if you do not like something and believe it is inappropriate or don't think you can deliver on a request. However, boundaries, like trust itself, can become tools of control and abuse. Never set boundaries that have the purpose of controlling your partner.

Respect Your Partner

One of the most important ways of building trust is to show your partner respect. Meet her needs, and don't put her down. Never belittle or look at her with condescension or contempt. Unfortunately, sometimes we are prone to lash out at people we are close to. This conveys a lack of respect that will destroy trust. Remember that every time you treat your partner in a way that breaches a basic level of respect, you will damage the connection of trust you have—and if you treat her with respect, you will build it.

Communicate Effectively

One more way to build trust in a relationship is to communicate effectively and express your feelings in a helpful way. Listen with empathy, and talk without shouting, verbally attacking, or shutting down the conversation. Review Chapter 18 for more discussion on peaceful communications and read Chapter 24 for skills that will enhance trust.

Summary

Intimate relationships are meant to be based on faith and trust. As noted above, the Golden Rule of Matthew 7:12 is a great summary of the importance of trust: "So in everything, do to others what you would have them do to you, for this sums up the Law and the Prophets."

Hopefully, actions based on the principles discussed above will move you toward transforming yourself, living according to the Golden Rule, and maintaining trust between you and your partner. Sometimes, however, trust has been demolished so badly that nothing sems to work. If this occurs, remember that you can control only yourself, and you should not try to control her. Nothing justifies or excuses further abuse of your partner.

Sometimes things just don't work and everyone needs to get beyond them. Review Chapter 14, Reconciliation, for some ideas on whether you should make further attempts to address trust issues with your partner, or go your separate ways in peace.

TRUST

Questions for Reflection or Group Study

1. Who do you trust? Why? (Do not include yourself.)

2. What are some qualities of someone you trust?

3. Explain how the following can become tools of control and abuse.

   Trust

   Boundaries

4. List things you have seen people do that:

   a. Build trust:

   b. Destroy trust:

   c. Rebuild trust

TRUST

5. How do you think the Golden Rule relates to trust?

6. Complete the following chart by listing specific action items you can do in each category to become more trustworthy.

	Action Item
1. Honesty	
2. Reliability	
3. Self-respect	
4. Boundaries	
5. Respect	
6. Communicate	

> **Personal Reflection**
>
> Which of the learning objectives for this chapter is most important to you in stopping abuse and transforming your life? Why?

CHAPTER 24

Working with Your Partner

Learning Objectives

After completing this chapter, you should be able to:
- Explain five basic approaches for dealing with day-to-day domestic issues.
- Foster win-win, interest based, problem solving that focuses on mutually beneficial solutions that support your partner's interests.
- Separate problems caused by your abuse from other domestic problems and focus separately on each of them.
- Understand that doing things suggested in other parts of this book will help you choose nonabusive behavior and prepare to work with your partner to address her interests.

MOST FAMILIES AND COUPLES ARE FACED with problems.

- They seem never to have enough money to make ends meet.
- One or the other is having a health problem.
- A child is doing poorly in school and seems to be going in the wrong direction.
- An aging parent needs more care.
- Partners disagree on where to live, or how to parent, or any number of other subjects.
- The primary provider loses his or her job.
- And on and on.

Do you and your partner have disagreements and problems such as these: problems that are normal in most households—not caused by your abuse but probably made worse by it? If so, what should you do to address them?

Martin Luther King, Jr., said in his letter from a Birmingham jail in April 1963, "We are caught in an inescapable network of mutuality, tied in a single garment of destiny. Whatever affects one directly, affects all . . ."

Most domestic problems, while different than the broad and pervasive problems Dr. King was addressing, are similar in one important way: "Whatever affects one, affects all." Most problems affect the entire family, and all need to work together to address them. An abuser needs to stop abusing and fix himself, and also do his best to work together with his partner to address the "normal" issues that arise in a domestic relationship.

Concepts of people working together are important in the Bible, beginning with the story of Adam and Eve, "united and of one flesh." Ecclesiastes 4:9 tells us, "Two are better than one, because they have a good return for their labor." And 1 Thessalonians 5:11 teaches, "Therefore encourage one another and build up each other, just as you are in fact doing."

When domestic partners work together, each person acknowledges that whatever affects one, affects all. They work together in their combined best interest and the interest of their loved ones. Both partners support one another, and each supports their combined interest.

To work with your partner, you need to let go of the idea of always being in control, and always winning or getting everything you want: attitudes that nearly always lead to continuing problems, unhappiness, and little to offer either party. Instead you need to accept the idea that all involved can benefit from working together to solve the day-to-day problems that occur in all families.

How you work with your partner will depend on your particular situation: for example, whether there are age or expertise differences; whether you are married, living together or apart, or have or do not have children; and numerous other factors that determine how people can best help and support one another. However, some basic principles apply in all situations. Three important ones for you are discussed briefly below.

WORKING WITH YOUR PARTNER

Stop Your Abusive Behavior

We noted in Chapter 1 that abuse involves coercive and controlling behavior, where an abuser intends to restrain or dominate by force, intimidation, or threat. Abusers typically are controlling and manipulative, and believe they have a right to be in charge of all aspects of a relationship. Such beliefs typically inform their handling of common domestic challenges, problems, and disagreements.

An abuser usually adopts a "competition" or controlling approach to such issues. He tries to get all he can for himself, as though he were buying a used car. He always tries to have the upper hand and benefit himself. He usually wins because he has the power, and the willingness to use it. His partner usually loses. For example, he insists his partner do all the household chores, or that she stay with the kids while he goes out with friends. The control element of such actions is the essence of abuse. It nearly always causes problems or makes them worse.

On the other hand, issues can be addressed in ways that are not controlling or abusive, and that avoid or minimize problems between you and your partner. Such approaches will vary with the circumstances, but may include one or more of the following:

- Avoiding: You conclude that objecting to what she did is not worth the effort or risk, so you ignore it and do nothing. (She spends more for your child's toy than you think she should, but you can afford it so you don't even mention the subject.)

- Accommodating: You disagree but decide that the problem isn't of great importance, so you mention it to your partner but go along with her doing what she wants. (You discuss the price of the toy, but are agreeable to her buying it.)

- Compromising: You try to make peace by "splitting the baby." Each wins something, but each also loses something. (The two of you have argued about household chores. You split them and allocate roughly half of them to each of you.)

- Collaborating: You work to satisfy both your needs. You often are able to find a solution where everyone wins. (The two of you work together to paint your house and use the savings to finance a trip both of you have wanted.)

Using these approaches to address issues without being abusive will minimize your problems. For those problems that do continue, consider the lessons presented in the preceding chapters. If you do the things suggested in those lessons, you are likely to get beyond your abusive behavior and attitudes and work with you partner. If you don't do them, effective problem solving is unlikely. In particular, read or reread the chapters dealing with the following key matters as you consider how you can work with your partner to address issues you are facing:

- Take responsibility for leading the effort toward an appropriate solution to your problems. (Chapter 6)

- Deal with any anger or substance abuse problems that, while not causing your abuse, may make the problems worse and interfere with your working together. (Chapter 15 and 16)

- Communicate positively and effectively, emphasizing effective listening. (Chapter 28)

- Empathize with your partner. (Chapter 6 and 7)

- Be trustworthy. (Chapter 23)

Behaving as discussed in these and other chapters will not guarantee success, as much will depend on the situation. However, doing so will help you stop the abuse and set the stage for proceeding to effectively address your problems.

Address Interests (Seek Win-Win)

If there is a significant problem or difference with your partner or within your family that needs to be addressed, you will need to decide how best to work with her, while respecting her opinions and understanding her perspective. How you work together will vary according to the circumstances, but you can bet that avoiding a win-lose competition, and instead working together in a win-win effort that addresses the needs of all involved is most likely to be the best approach. The following section describes a win-lose approach, and the one after it discusses win-win problem-solving.

Avoid Win-Lose (Competition)

As an abuser, your main objective in many problem-solving situations no doubt is to be in control, to have your way, to win the contest. You frequently take fixed positions and insist on them: my way or the highway. You use your power to control the situation and insist that the abused partner give in. Your victim may give in, out of fear or to keep the peace, but little or no mutuality is involved. You benefit to the detriment of your partner. You win and she loses. Bitter disputes may result and further damage future relationships between you.

Let's consider an example of a competitive approach where one partner wins and the other loses. Bob and Jane lived in a nice home in a nice middle-class subdivision. Bob was afraid he would lose his job, and with taxes increasing every year, he came to believe they couldn't live there anymore. He told Jane they needed to move. Jane liked where she was, and wanted to stay. After a few very heated discussions on the subject, Bob took control, sold the house, and signed a contract for a less expensive, zero lot-line condo in another part of town. None of Jane's needs were met. She was devastated, and she threatened to leave him. Bob got his way and "won." Jane lost.

Sometimes what starts as a competition where each party aims to win ends with a compromise: the parties give in and simply split the difference, with neither person being satisfied. In a compromise, each wins some and loses some, but the more one gets, the less the other gets. While the result is often better than win-lose, those involved often do not feel good about it, as their needs are still not satisfied.

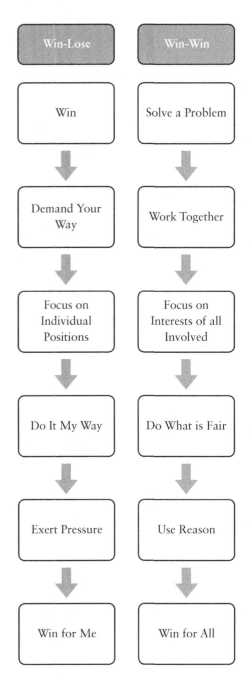

Foster Win-Win (Interest Based)

Bob and Jane could have worked together to find a solution based on respect and nonviolence, where both won. In win-win—sometimes called interest based—problem solving, the people involved work together to find a solution of their problem that supports both of their needs and interests.

The chart above introduces win-win problem solving and compares this strategy with win-lose.

Interests are the underlying reasons why people care about the issue being considered: the needs, desires, concerns, and fears that are important to each side. In the case of Jane and Bob, Bob's interest was financial. He wanted to reduce the monthly payments. Jane's interests were different. She wanted a house with a yard, and she wanted its location to continue to be near her ailing mother. When they sold the house and bought the condo, Bob's interest was supported. Jane's were not.

The aim of a win-win solution is to consider the interests—the real wants and needs—of all involved and develop solutions that to the extent possible address them. Sometimes this results in a compromise where neither gets all they want, but both get something they can live with; and at other times they are able to work together and expand the "size of the pie" so that the solution provides both with all they want. In Bob's and Jane's case, Bob could have worked with her and purchased a smaller, fixer-upper with a yard in a less expensive area near Jane's mother. This would have met both their interests and given each of them a win.

You will have to decide how best to work with your partner, and the answer will vary according to the circumstances. It's clear, however, that a win-win, interest-based approach to resolving problems and working together holds the best chance for a mutually beneficial—happy, cooperative, productive—relationship in which both parties can usually have the best chance of having most of their needs met.

Separate the People from the Problem

Working with another person nearly always requires some type of problem solving, discussion, and/or negotiation that moves toward an understanding as to how different things will be handled. Separating two types of issues will help you decide what to do in various situations.

Identify the Substantive Issues

Substantive issues are those that deal with real, tangible, living interests, such as money, resources, living conditions, or other matters that need to be resolved by the partners. These issues often involve fixed or limited resources that may need to be divided, and may present an opportunity for the parties to work together in a win-win approach to "expand the size of the pie" and allow each to get what they need. Substantive issues are generally fact based, logical, easier to understand.

Acknowledge the Relationship or People Issues

Relationship issues involve things that are not tangible, but nevertheless are critical to the process of living and working together with your partner. They include matters involving personal peculiarities, strengths and weaknesses, needs and wants, and how you treat one another. Examples might include how you communicate, your intimate relations, how you resolve problems, personal habits, the level of trust between you, and such. In your situation, the most important relationship issue probably concerns your abuse of your partner.

Relationship problems often involve difficult emotions such as fear, anger, distrust, and anxiety—problems caused or made worse by abuse—and present problems of perception, emotion, and communication. What is "real" is interpreted differently by your partner and you. When you and your partner have problems with your relationship, particularly involving your abuse of her, solving substantive problems may be very difficult to achieve.

Separate People Issues from Substantive Issues

To deal with the two different types of concerns you need to separate the people from the problems, which means to the extent possible separating relationship issues, particularly your abuse, from substantive issues, and dealing with them independently. Unless relationship issues are separated, emotions get intertwined with the substantive issues and make both harder to deal with.

To successfully separate the people from the problem, consider the following tips.

- Take responsibility for your abuse and acknowledge what you have done. Don't try to deny, minimize, rationalize or blame someone else for your actions.

- Remember that you are in a long-term relationship, and you will need to work with your partner in the future on a foundation of personal safety, free of controlling and threatening behavior. Empathize with her, and how your abuse has affected her. Try to give first priority to your relationship. For example, you may need to suggest addressing a recent incident when you abused her before you discuss a substantive problem such as financial concerns.

- Model win-win problem solving by not controlling or dominating the discussion, and instead suggesting "separating the people from the problem" and respecting her response.

- Model respectful behavior and don't cause additional personal problems, regardless of how you feel you are being treated. Don't insult your partner. Don't allow yourself to try to dominate or control the process.

- Try to see yourself and your partner as allies, working together on the same team against a mutual problem. This minimizes the tendency for you to villainize her and makes it easier for you to be more accommodating and to collaborate with her and resolve issues in healthy, nonviolent ways.

Summary

All families and relationships have problems. When interests are great and emotions are high, it's easy for a problem-solving session with your partner to become an opportunity for you to abuse her again. In the end, such development will only lead to lousy decisions that fail to solve the problem, and to a worse relationship. Instead, if you stop your controlling and abusive behavior, foster a win-win process, and try to separate the people from the problem, you can take the lead in a problem-solving process that will be more likely to solve your substantive problems in a safe and nonviolent way.

WORKING WITH YOUR PARTNER

Questions for Reflection or Group Study

1. What do you learn about working together from the quote of Dr. King and the Scripture in the introductory narrative for this chapter?

2. List several of your needs or interests.

3. List what you believe are several of your partner's needs or interests.

4. On the chart below mark an "S" to indicate a substantive issue and an "R" to indicate a relationship issue. List your main interest and your partner's main interest relating to each issue, taking care to honestly consider your partner's interest and avoid gender stereotypes.

	S or R	My Main Interest	Partner's Main Interest
1. Money			
2. Sex			
3. Use of Time			
4. Parenting			
5. Religion			
6. Privacy			
7. Extended Family			
8. Living Conditions			

5. What do you learn from the exercise in 4 above?

6. What should you do to "separate the people from the problem" when you are solving problems with your partner?

> ### Personal Reflection
>
> Which of the learning objectives for this chapter is most important to you in stopping abuse and transforming your life? Why?

PART FOUR
Future Plans

PLAN TO DO RIGHT

CHAPTER 25

Goals

> ### Learning Objectives
>
> After completing this chapter, you should be able to:
> - See goals as a powerful process for thinking about your future, and for motivating you to do what is appropriate to make it the best it can be.
> - Understand SMART: goals that are specific, measurable, attainable, relevant, and time bound/trackable.
> - Set thoughtful and purposeful goals that describe how you will stop abusing and transform your life.

YOU HAVE NOW READ *STOP ABUSE AND TRANSform Your Life* and considered many questions about yourself and your abuse. Hopefully you have learned a great deal that will help you transform your life and stop abusing others.

Now—your challenge is doing it! What do you do and when do you do it? What are your priorities? How do you use what you've learned to transform your life and restore peace? How do you stay motivated to make these changes?

These are not easy questions. You need to be thoughtful and purposeful in answering them, and setting goals is a great way to do this. Goal setting is a powerful process for thinking about your future, and for motivating you to do what is appropriate to make it the best it can be. The process helps you choose where you want to go in life and where to concentrate your efforts. Setting goals allows you to plan your life and feel a sense of accomplishment and self-worth when you have succeeded.

Processes for using goals can vary, and a number of websites contain good information about establishing and using them. A powerful, commonly used approach is the use of SMART goals—written goals and objectives that are:

S – Specific
M – Measurable
A – Attainable
R – Relevant
T – Time bound/Trackable

This approach involves setting a very few overarching goals that are broad in scope and almost aspirational, supported by several more limited objectives that, if accomplished, will fulfill the goals. You may wish to set goals and objectives in a number of areas of your life, such as career, financial, or others, and this should not discourage you from doing so. However, completion and use of the following will help you develop and attain meaningful progress in stopping abuse and transforming your life to one that fosters peace.

Goals and Objectives

Overarching Goal

I will develop a relationship with my spouse/partner that is honestly described as follows:

Description of relationship:

This goal will be completed by:

I will know that this goal has been accomplished because:

Implementing Objectives

1. I will avoid abusive behavior as follows: (List at least two specific examples of each behavior to be avoided)

Behavior to Be Avoided	How I Will Measure/Know It's Avoided
1.	
2.	

2. I have reviewed the topics discussed in Part Two: responsibility, accountability, confession, forgiveness, restitution, and reconciliation. I will pursue the following objectives relating to (at least two) of these topics in an effort to accomplish my overarching goal stated above.

Objective to Be Accomplished	When to Be Accomplished	How I Will Measure/ Know It's Accomplished
1.		
2.		

GOALS

3. I have reviewed the topics discussed in Part Three involving anger, substance abuse, communication, sexual respect, fatherhood, trust and respect, and working together. I will pursue the following objectives relating to (at least two) of these topics in an effort to accomplish my overarching goal stated above.

Objective to Be Accomplished	When to Be Accomplished	How I Will Measure/ Know It's Accomplished
1.		
2.		

I will review these objectives, measure progress, and update as appropriate on the following dates:

_____   _____

_____   _____

_____   _____

Signature   Date

Appendix

Information for Group Facilitators

The Roadmap

MANY ABUSERS STOP ABUSING FOR A WHILE and then return to their former lifestyle. *Stop Abuse and Transform Your Life* aims to help them do more than stop abusive behavior. It aims to help them transform—totally reorient—their lives from ones involving control and violence to ones of peace and love.

Like other social problems, domestic abuse is a multifaceted problem that requires a multifaceted solution. Domestic violence affects and is affected by many aspects of people's lives: physical, psychological, mental, their life stories, and their faith. And personal transformation requires an overall change in many such aspects of the person's being. Such a change is described in the Bible in Romans 12:2, "Do not conform to the pattern of this world, but be transformed by the renewing of your mind. Then you will be able to test and approve what God's will is—his good, pleasing and perfect will."

Fostering such change requires one to deal with people as a system of interacting, interrelated parts that comprise the whole, and to use programs that consider all relevant parts of the system. *Stop Abuse and Transform Your Life* takes this approach. It considers life as a journey, and includes discussion of a broad range of issues aiming to help abusive men stop their abuse and change their life journeys. It presents a journey in four parts.

PART ONE: ABUSE, YOU, AND GOD helps abusers understand the problem of abuse, their own actions, and the role of faith in helping them change. It emphasizes their need to stop abusive behavior immediately.

PART TWO: RESTORE PEACE helps abusers make a U-turn in their lives. It presents tools to help restore or improve relationships that have been broken by past abuse, if doing so is feasible and appropriate.

PART THREE: MAINTAIN PEACE helps abusers handle future forks in the road, make the right choices, and live a life of peace without abusing.

PART FOUR: FUTURE PLANS helps abusers develop plans for doing the right things to continue to live lives of peace without abusing others.

Principles from five different sources underlie these discussions.

Accepted Batterer Intervention Programs

This book does not start from scratch or attempt to invent a totally new process. Instead, it includes many principles that have been used in helping men stop abuse and are the basis of most existing recognized battering intervention programs. In particular, the writers found *Education Groups for Men who Batter: The Duluth Model* by Ellen Pence and Michael Paymar (Springer Publishing Company, New York, 1993) and *Alternatives to Domestic Violence: A Homework Manual for Battering Intervention Groups* by Kevin A Fall and Shareen Howard (Routledge, New York, 2012) to provide helpful information.

Certifying Agencies

Stop Abuse and Transform Your Life addresses the principles raised by BIP programs in a number of states, and is approved for use in accredited BIP programs in Texas. Each program administrator should ensure that their program meets all appropriate requirements.

Faith

Faith, religion, and spirituality often are treated as equal and interchangeable concepts. In this book, we consider them as different but related. We consider faith as a person's belief and trust in a Higher Power. Faith, in turn, is the foundation of religion, one's system of belief about a deity, often involving rituals, a code of ethics, and a philosophy of life; and of spirituality, our conscious self-recognition that we are more than just a body, and also are a soul with infinite

APPENDIX

potential. In this context, faith involves "knowing," religion involves "doing," and spirituality involves "being." With faith as a foundation, religion and spirituality can be seen as structures that help an individual avoid abuse and live his or her life in peace. (This model draws heavily on *Faith, Spirituality, and Religion: A Model for Understanding the Difference*.[18]

The authors of this book are all life-long Christians. Therefore, without in any way diminishing other beliefs, it presents a Christian perspective on stopping abuse and transforming the life of the abuser. It considers God to be our Higher Power, and uses the Bible for guidance in suggesting ways for men to transform their lives to avoid abuse, focus on peace and love, and attain their full spiritual potential. The book does not proselytize, try to convert readers to a particular theology, or dismiss or minimize the teachings of any of the other great world religions—which we suspect are supportive of the principles presented here.

The authors acknowledge that the Bible contains stories of violence against women and is often seen to have a patriarchal bent that endorses male dominance over women. In addition, religious people have too often inappropriately encouraged battered women to stay in abusive relationships and try to be "better wives," while helping batterers justify their actions because women are to be "subject to men in all things."

However, the conclusion is inevitable that when read holistically, the Bible condemns all domestic abuse and fosters love, respect, and gender equality. Readers are encouraged to celebrate those Scripture in which women serve as strong and courageous role models, and understand that, theologically and ethically, sexual and domestic violence are wrong and constitute sin—the physical, psychological, and spiritual violation of one person by another. If selective reading of Scripture is avoided and it is considered in the fuller context of history, ethics, theology, and doctrine, one concludes that Scripture condemns abusive behavior, and provides tools for dealing with its consequences as well as avoiding it in the future.

Stories

Stop Abuse and Transform Your Life encourages abusers to look deeply at their own life stories—perhaps both as victims of abuse and as perpetrators of it—in order to help them understand how experiences from their childhood probably have contributed to their abusing as an adult. Studies have found that men who were exposed to domestic violence as children are three to four times more likely to perpetrate intimate partner violence as adults than men who were not. This book suggests abusers need to understand and address this fact if they are to stop abuse permanently and transform their lives. It acknowledges and addresses the likely role of past abuse by emphasizing life stories, while making it clear that although past abuse may be a contributing factor in current abuse, it cannot in any way be used as an excuse for or justification of any abuse of others.

Restorative Justice

The criminal justice system in the United States has historically been based largely on the idea of retribution, which focuses on punishing offenders and giving them their just deserts. Restorative justice, an alternate or complementary system that has been evolving over the last several decades, focuses on repairing the harm caused by crime and rehabilitating offenders through reconciliation with victims and the community at large. It has been described by Howard Zehr, often considered the godfather of restorative justice in the US, as "a process to involve, to the extent possible, those who have a stake in a specific offense and to collectively identify and address harms, needs, and obligations, in order to heal and put things as right as possible."

Two key ideas of restorative justice that are directly applicable to issues of battering and abuse are: (1) crime (and abuse) causes harm and justice requires repairing that harm; (2) a goal is to cause transformation, or fundamental changes in people, relationships and communities.

Most people—abusers and victims alike—have experienced periods of peace and well-being in their lives and in their relationships with others. If they have abused others, they have destroyed much of this peace. To repair the harm and transform their lives, abusers need to deal with this past and restore the feeling of peace and well-being to their victims as well as themselves. This requires efforts such as sharing by those involved while also focusing on harm, calling for confession, endorsing forgiveness, expecting repentance, making restitution, and striving for some form of reconciliation.

APPENDIX

Abusers typically have hurt others in ways not greatly different from the behavior of many incarcerated persons, may be feeling the effects of psychological "imprisonment" because of their actions, and probably need to deal with similar issues as those who are incarcerated. Therefore, many of this book's key concepts are modeled on the book, *Restoring Peace: Using Lessons from Prison to Mend Broken Relationships*, used as the basic curriculum with great success in the Texas based restorative justice prison ministry, Bridges to Life. There are obvious differences between incarcerated individuals and abusers in the free world. However, BTL's amazing growth, largely organic and unplanned, and positive recidivism results suggest that its principles will help abusers look back at the hurt they have caused others, make things right with them, and restore peace to both their lives. Therefore, "PART TWO: Restore Peace" is largely based on the book, *Restoring Peace*, and learnings from the Bridges to Life restorative justice program.

Ideas for Group Study

Stop Abuse and Transform Your Life is intended for any man who is guilty of domestic abuse and is trying to beat it—trying to stop the abuse and transform his life—whether on his own initiative or as a requirement of the judicial system. In either case, the book may be read and studied individually or as part of a small group of men with similar issues, needs, and objectives.

Those reading the book individually should consider the suggestions under THIS BOOK IS YOUR ROADMAP in the INTRODUCTION. Those reading the book as part of a Batterers Intervention and Prevention Program (BIPP) or other group process should be expected to follow the Program's approach and procedures. The authors recommend a model generally along the following lines, subject of course to any state or other mandated requirements.

Group Sessions

Meet for approximately one and one-half hour, once a week in groups of up to ten men who are dealing with domestic violence. A facilitator or facilitators leads the group in discussion of the chapter assigned from *Stop Abuse and Transform Your Life*.

The learning process focuses on reading, writing, and dialogue. As preparation for each week's meeting, participants should do homework that is comprised of reading an assigned chapter from this book and writing answers to the questions that follow. At the day's meeting, facilitators should lead dialogue among participants in which they discuss the Questions for Reflection or Group Study, honestly share ideas, and listen to one another without trying to convince anyone of anything or make judgments about one another.

Participant Scheduling

Ideally, each group should be established with all group members starting at the same time and working together through the book, chapter by chapter in the book's sequence—starting with Chapter 1 and culminating with Chapter 25.

If it is necessary to conduct an open enrollment program where participants can join a group at any time, the following approach is suggested:

- Require each participant to read the narrative and complete the homework in PART ONE of *Stop Abuse and Transform Your Life* and discuss it privately with a facilitator sufficient to indicate a basic understanding of the thrust of the program to follow.

- Have each participant start group sessions on an odd number chapter if feasible. As a general rule, the odd numbered chapters explore some aspect of domestic abuse and/or certain important principles, and the even chapters explore more specific ways participants can use these principles to change their lives.

- Have the participant progress with the group through all the book chapters in PART ONE, TWO, and THREE, (Chapters 1-24) including a more detailed discussion of PART ONE when those chapters are scheduled in their normal course. For each chapter, participants should do the following homework:

    – Read the narrative for the appropriate class session.

    – Write answers to the assigned homework questions for the day's session.

APPENDIX

- Prepare to discuss their answers and engage in dialog when their group meets.

- In an early session, each participant should tell his story to his small group, using Chapter 2 as a guide.

- Each participant should complete PART FOUR, Chapter 25 and discuss it in group after all other chapters have been completed.

Program administrators may wish to spend more than one session on certain topics (such as the accountability statement of Chapter 8) and less that a complete session on other topics to best meet the needs of participants and the approving authority.

Confidentiality

The importance of confidentiality concerning group discussions cannot be overstated, as confidentiality promotes an atmosphere in which participants can be more open and honest. Confidentiality is one of the program's "group covenants." Each group member should be advised of this requirement in advance and required to covenant to keep whatever is shared within the confines of the group in order to provide the atmosphere necessary for openness and truth. Anyone who violates this requirement of confidentiality, even unintentionally, should normally be dismissed from the program.

Under certain circumstances a facilitator must disclose information that has been shared within a group. If this is your case, participants normally should be advised in advance.

Writing in this document responding to any of the Questions for Reflection or Group Study is an effort at self-analysis and behavior improvement by the participant and should be considered privileged and strictly confidential. However, under certain circumstances an adverse party in a legal proceeding may attempt to require access to the writing. If a participant is concerned about possible legal implications of an answer, consider suggesting that he write that answer on a separate paper for use in group and separate handling thereafter. Participants may be encouraged to discuss a more personal application in group discussions.

The Faith Factor

Stop Abuse and Transform Your Life suggests a faith-based approach that considers belief in God as important to success in stopping domestic violence. However, facilitators should avoid Bible teaching, "preaching," proselytizing, or trying to convert participants to a particular view of religion. While the book is presented from a Christian point of view, often citing Scripture and the teaching of Jesus and his apostles, discussions should be ecumenical, and a particular religious belief—or even a professed belief in God—should not be required for participation. Participants should be encouraged to learn some important lessons from the teachings of scripture, regardless of the theology involved.

Facilitators should emphasize spirituality in the deepest sense of belonging and inclusiveness rather than any particular dogma or set of religious practices. Facilitators are encouraged to recognize and acknowledge that the Bible came into being in a culture of male dominance, and over the years has largely been interpreted by men, from a male perspective, often in ways that seem to justify the subordination, perhaps even abuse, of women. However, theologians also have pointed out that the Bible supports conclusions such as the value and dignity of women, opposition to male dominance, and help for women in recognizing their true condition and having a vision of a positive future. Faith is based on equality, where men and women have different roles, but are equal human beings with roles of equal importance.

Endnotes

[1] Article by Hannah Dellinger. Dec 29, 2019. *Houston Chronicle*, Houston, Texas. https://www.pressreader.com/usa/houston-chronicle-sunday/20191229/281590947480769

[2] Centers for Disease Control and Prevention. "Preventing Intimate Partner Violence Fact Sheet." https://www.cdc.gov/violenceprevention/intimatepartnerviolence/fastfact.html

[3] Ibid.

[4] Ibid.

[5] Kraut Law Group. Los Angeles DUI Attorney Blog. November 17, 2019. "The Generational Nature of Domestic Violence, and How to Break the Cycle." https://www.losangelesduiattorneyblog.com/the-generational-nature-of-domestic-violence-and-how-to-break-the-cycle

[6] *The Courier* of Montgomery County. Mar 14, 2017. https://www.yourconroenews.com/neighborhood/moco/news/article/Willis-man-gets-15-years-for-slapping-girlfriend-11000837.php

[7] L. Gregory Jones. *Embodying Forgiveness: A Theological Analysis*. Grand Rapids: W. B. Eerdmans Publishing Co. 1995.

[8] Harvard Health Publishing, Harvard Medical School. "The power of forgiveness." February 12, 2021. https://www.health.harvard.edu/mind-and-mood/the-power-of-forgiveness

[9] Jones, *Embodying Forgiveness*.

[10] "Mississippi leaders: Lawmaker should resign if he hit wife" by Emily Wagster Pettus. *Seattle Times*, May 22, 2019. https://www.seattletimes.com/nation-world/nation/mississippi-leaders-lawmaker-should-resign-if-he-hit-wife/

[11] Jennifer A. Bennice and Patricia A. Resick, "MARITAL RAPE: History, Research, and Practice." *JSTOR*, Vol. 4, No. 3. www.jstor.org/stable/26636357

[12] Domestic Violence Resource Centre Victoria. "Ann's story." https://www.dvrcv.org.au/stories/anns-story

[13] Ellen Pence and Michael Paymar. *Education Groups for Men who Batter: The Duluth Model.* New York: Springer Publishing Company, 1993.

[14] Jacquelyn C. Campbell and Peggy Alford. "The Dark Consequences of Marital Rape." *The American Journal of Nursing*, Vol. 89, No. 7. July 1989. In *JSTOR*. www.jstor.org/stable/3426372

[15] Fergus Hogan and Máire O'Reilly, "Listening to children: Children's stories of domestic violence." Centre for Social and Family Research, Department of Applied Arts, Waterford Institute of Technology. October 2007.' https://www.womensaid.ie/assets/files/pdf/listening_to_children_childrens_stories_of_domestic_violence.pdf

[16] Ranjith Kumar. "Trust . . . A Small Story To Read With Big Message. . ." *CiteHR*. March 11, 2008. https://www.citehr.com/89599-trust-small-story-read-big-message.html

[17] "Archive of Stories, Stories for Preaching and Teaching." Fr. Tommy Lane, SSL, STD. http://www.frtommylane.com/stories.htm

[18] Lance Gargus, "A Little Girl and Her Father Were Crossing A Bridge." Faith Writers, 6.19.16. https://www.faithwriters.com/article-details.php?id=184516

About the Authors

KIRK BLACKARD, a graduate of Texas A&M and the University of Texas School of Law, is a retired Shell Oil Company executive. He is a long-time volunteer, board member, and former chairman of the board of Bridges To Life, a large restorative justice prison ministry headquartered in Texas. Kirk has written nine books on conflict, restorative justice, and related matters.

FRANCESCA BLACKARD is a partner at McClure Law Group, where she exclusively practices family law. She holds a Bachelor of Arts degree from DePaul University, a Doctor of Jurisprudence degree from New York Law School, and has been recognized as a *D Magazine* Best Family Lawyer. Francesca has professional and volunteer experience working with abused women and men. She is married to Drew Blackard (Kirk's son) and is the mother of twins.

ALBERT CHAGOYA is executive director at the Addicare Batterers Intervention Prevention Program in Dallas, Texas. He has a Bachelor of Science degree from The University of Texas at Arlington, with concentrations in political science and criminal justice. Albert has extensive experience in maintaining program TDCJ-CJAD accreditation standards; group supervision and facilitation of English and Spanish BIPP Programs; fostering relationships with domestic violence courts, probation, and Child Protective Services; and providing domestic violence training for governmental agencies and other Battering Intervention and Prevention Program (BIPP) programs.

Index

Accountability, 60, 78-84, 88-93, 107, 108, 157
   Accountability statement, 95
   For future actions, 90
   For past actions, 91
   To self, 81
   To God, 79
   To others, 88-93
Adam and Eve, 33, 79, 280
Alcohol, 15, 176-181,
Anger, 165-170
   Anger management, 170
   Cause and effect, 22, 167
Apology, 47, 99, 107, 109, 110, 157
Assumptions, 192, 199, 206
Attitude, 49, 52, 134, 167, 198, 245

Behavior, 124, 170, 181, 230
   Learned, 48, 177
Beliefs, 10, 49, 53, 166, 168, 170, 177, 199, 245
Biases, 73, 193, 199

Bible, 4, 32, 33, 34, 37, 52, 79, 166, 195, 214
Blame, 10, 52, 55, 64, 79, 100, 109, 244, 285

Cause/effect, 60, 61, 167, 341, 262
Causes of abuse, 13, 58, 180, 237
Center for Disease Control and Prevention, 2
Change, 9, 47, 52, 54, 65, 100, 119, 168, 170, 181
Children, 252-263
Choice, 22, 64, 71, 230, 79, 81, 83, 108, 134, 153, 179, 197, 227, 232, 271
Christian, 4, 11, 32, 71, 92, 100, 103, 206, 301
Commitment, 6, 55, 58, 83, 107, 156, 232
Communication, 114, 130, 151, 170, 273
   Abusive, 186-193
   Nonverbal, 189, 200

   Verbal, 188, 200
   Peaceful, 197-207
Communion, 100, 119, 133
Competition, 281, 283
Compromise, 283
Confession, 93, 118, 153
   How, 111
   Purpose, 99
   To others, 107-114
   To self and God, 98-103
   To a third party, 101
   When, 110
Confidentiality, 305
Conscience, 81-82, 132
Consequences, 14-15, 51, 61, 62, 65, 79, 120, 166, 230, 254
Context, 206
Control, 14, 32, 34, 50, 83, 155, 168, 271
Court, 23, 114, 128, 141, 259
Criminal law, 12, 215, 217, 220, 229, 302
Cry wolf, 232

David and Bathsheba, 60, 103, 240
Dialogue, 22-24, 101, 157, 206, 304
Digital abuse, 11, 51, 190, 62
Discipline, 247, 254, 260-263
Disrespect, 50, 244, 254
Domestic abuse, 9-16
Drugs, 16, 176-181, 218

Effects of abuse, 14, 61, 243, 135
Emotions, 73, 74, 83, 113, 119, 192, 193, 200, 202, 206, 285
    Emotional abuse, 10, 50
Empathy, 24, 54, 72-74, 83, 136, 157, 169, 198, 205, 258, 286
Entitlement, 50, 169, 229
Expectations, 90, 167, 202, 204, 262

Facilitators, 299
Faith, 4, 32-39, 79, 80, 230, 274, 300, 306
Family, 10, 13, 14, 15, 23, 39, 72, 152, 244, 252-263, 280
Fathers, 49, 62-63, 98, 121, 240-247, 252-257
Fear, 14, 145, 167, 222, 261, 269-270
Feedback, 54, 200, 203
Feelings, 10, 21, 22, 23, 24, 49, 73-74, 109, 131, 133, 170, 201, 234, 271
Forgiveness, 103, 118-136
    About forgiveness, 119, 128
    Forgiving others, 131, 153
    Forgiving yourself, 122
    God's forgiveness, 118-124,
    No forgiveness, 135
    Reconciliation, 133
Free will, 62, 63, 81, 92
Friend, 151, 255

Goals, 3, 37, 293-297
God, 11, 33, 35, 36, 71, 79, 102, 121, 124, 142, 253
God's law, 11, 229
Grace, 100, 121, 124
Heart, 47, 82, 102, 130, 234
Hippocratic oath, 109
Honesty, 11, 258, 268
Hostile home environment, 217-218
Houston Chronicle, 1, 159
Howard Zehr, 302
Human beings, 34, 62, 112, 123, 152, 169, 214, 219, 229
Human rights, 11, 12, 217, 229
Humanity, 34, 113, 152, 157
Humility, 52, 112-113, 134, 155

I statement, 203
If only questions, 63

Journal, 5, 25-26, 102, 134
Judging, 24, 78, 218
Justification, 21, 55, 178, 179, 302
    Blaming, 55, 64, 102, 109, 218, 270
    Denying, 51, 55, 64, 109
    Minimizing, 37, 51, 55, 64, 109
    Rationalizing, 51, 55, 64, 109

INDEX

Learning, 80, 187, 192, 241, 304
Listening, 23, 73, 82, 110, 157, 187, 191, 198-201, 206, 246, 258, 304
Love, 35, 71-72, 83, 153, 169, 228, 259
    Need love, 36, 71
    Gift love, 36, 71
    Agape love, 71, 72, 230

Male entitlement, 228, 247, 301
Manasseh, 118, 123
Martin Luther King Jr, 281
Media, 11, 190, 215, 229
Mercy, 121, 134
Moral codes, 37, 92
    Ten commandments, 37, 92, 243
    Sermon on the mount, 37, 92
    Golden rule, 38. 92
Moral values, 82, 258
Mutuality, 89, 214, 156, 227, 269, 286, 252-263

Objectives, 198, 294

Partner, 2, 9, 12, 23, 51, 72-73, 107, 199-202, 216, 253, 256, 273
Pornography, 190, 215, 229
Power, 10, 13, 49, 129, 154, 178, 202, 219, 228, 257, 269, 281, 283
Pray, 102, 151, 153, 155, 158
Prodigal son, 98-99
Programs, 3, 170, 179-181, 299
Punishment, 61, 203, 247, 260, 263

Rape, 61, 214-215, 220-222
Reconciliation, 133, 150-158, 231, 233-234, 302
Religion, 4, 32, 35, 47, 267, 300
Remorse, 47, 48, 121, 134, 232
Repentance, 47-55, 135, 153
Respect, 12, 54, 71, 79, 80, 89, 113, 134, 198, 213, 258, 236
    Sexual respect, 227-235
Responsibility, 13, 21, 60-65, 70-74, 99, 112, 145, 153, 157, 179, 205, 285

Unhealthy responses, 64
    Accepting, 65
Restitution, 135, 140-146
    Direct, 145
    Symbolic, 145
    Community, 146
Restorative justice, 302
Ripple effect, 15, 61, 62, 135, 241, 243
Road map, 5, 153
Role model, 243, 255-257, 260
Root cause, 167, 168, 170, 179, 180

Self-respect, 272
Self, 100, 119, 121, 123, 143, 258
Selfish, 50, 52, 112, 113, 169, 230
Servant leader, 257-259
Sexual abuse, 11, 51, 143, 212-222
    Coercive sexual activity, 219
    Hostile home environment, 217
    Reproductive coercion, 220
    Sexual violence, 221
    Unwanted sexual contact, 218
Sexual ethics, 213
    Consent, 216

Sexual respect, 227-235
   Repentance, 229
   Forgiveness, 231
   Restitution, 233
Shalom, 38
Sir Matthew Hale, 214
SMART goals, 293
Social media, 11, 190
Solitude, 101
Spiritual abuse, 10, 11, 21, 51, 151
Stalking, 9, 190
Stories, 20-26, 33, 37, 61, 98, 111, 124, 157, 301
Substance abuse, 2, 176-181, 282
Sympathy, 72

Transform, 4, 48, 52-55, 103, 119, 121, 142, 146, 153, 205, 293, 302
Triggers of abuse, 177, 178, 242
Trust, 36, 74, 91, 109, 132, 155, 23, 204-205, 227, 231, 267-274

U-turn, 3, 4, 5, 6, 47, 54, 135, 299

Victim, 16, 54, 64, 72, 100, 110, 119, 141, 144, 214, 222, 231, 271, 283

Verbal abuse, 10, 50, 187

Whole person, 143-144
Why analysis, 62, 167
Win/win, 158, 282-284
Words, 10, 34, 60, 110, 114, 187-188, 198, 205, 206
Working together, 23, 255, 279-286

Zacchaeus, 141

Made in the USA
Coppell, TX
17 June 2023